OPPOSING VIEWPOINTS®

MASS MEDIA

Other Books of Related Interest

OPPOSING VIEWPOINTS®

MASS MEDIA

William Dudley, *Book Editor*

Bruce Glassman, *Vice President*
Bonnie Szumski, *Publisher*
Helen Cothran, *Managing Editor*

OPPOSING
VIEWPOINTS®
SERIES

GREENHAVEN
PRESS®

THOMSON

★
™

GALE

San Diego • Detroit • New York • San Francisco • Cleveland
New Haven, Conn. • Waterville, Maine • London • Munich

THOMSON
─────★───── ™
GALE

For more information, contact
Greenhaven Press
27500 Drake Rd.
Farmington Hills, MI 48331-3535
Or you can visit our Internet site at http://www.gale.com

Cover credit: © Brand X Pictures

LIBRARY OF CONGRESS CATALOGING-IN-PUBLICATION DATA
Mass media : opposing viewpoints / William Dudley, book editor.
p. cm. — (Opposing viewpoints series)
Includes bibliographical references and index.
ISBN 0-7377-2242-8 (lib. : alk. paper) — ISBN 0-7377-2243-6 (pbk. : alk. paper)
1. Mass media—United States. I. Dudley, William, 1964– . II. Opposing
viewpoints series (Unnumbered)
P92.U5M276 2005
302.23'0973—dc22   2004042401

"Congress shall make
no law... abridging the
freedom of speech, or of
the press."

First Amendment to the U.S. Constitution

The basic foundation of our democracy is the First
Amendment guarantee of freedom of expression.
The Opposing Viewpoints Series is dedicated to the
concept of this basic freedom and the idea that it is
more important to practice it than to enshrine it.

Contents

Why Consider Opposing Viewpoints?

"The only way in which a human being can make some approach to knowing the whole of a subject is by hearing what can be said about it by persons of every variety of opinion and studying all modes in which it can be looked at by every character of mind. No wise man ever acquired his wisdom in any mode but this."

John Stuart Mill

In our media-intensive culture it is not difficult to find differing opinions. Thousands of newspapers and magazines and dozens of radio and television talk shows resound with differing points of view. The difficulty lies in deciding which opinion to agree with and which "experts" seem the most credible. The more inundated we become with differing opinions and claims, the more essential it is to hone critical reading and thinking skills to evaluate these ideas. Opposing Viewpoints books address this problem directly by presenting stimulating debates that can be used to enhance and teach these skills. The varied opinions contained in each book examine many different aspects of a single issue. While examining these conveniently edited opposing views, readers can develop critical thinking skills such as the ability to compare and contrast authors' credibility, facts, argumentation styles, use of persuasive techniques, and other stylistic tools. In short, the Opposing Viewpoints Series is an ideal way to attain the higher-level thinking and reading skills so essential in a culture of diverse and contradictory opinions.

In addition to providing a tool for critical thinking, Opposing Viewpoints books challenge readers to question their own strongly held opinions and assumptions. Most people form their opinions on the basis of upbringing, peer pressure, and personal, cultural, or professional bias. By reading carefully balanced opposing views, readers must directly confront new ideas as well as the opinions of those with whom they disagree. This is not to simplistically argue that everyone who reads opposing views will—or should—change his or her opinion. Instead, the series enhances readers' understanding of their own views by encouraging confrontation with opposing ideas. Careful examination of others' views can lead to the readers' understanding of the logical inconsistencies in their own opinions, perspective on why they hold an opinion, and the consideration of the possibility that their opinion requires further evaluation.

Evaluating Other Opinions

To ensure that this type of examination occurs, Opposing Viewpoints books present all types of opinions. Prominent spokespeople on different sides of each issue as well as well-known professionals from many disciplines challenge the reader. An additional goal of the series is to provide a forum for other, less known, or even unpopular viewpoints. The opinion of an ordinary person who has had to make the decision to cut off life support from a terminally ill relative, for example, may be just as valuable and provide just as much insight as a medical ethicist's professional opinion. The editors have two additional purposes in including these less known views. One, the editors encourage readers to respect others' opinions—even when not enhanced by professional credibility. It is only by reading or listening to and objectively evaluating others' ideas that one can determine whether they are worthy of consideration. Two, the inclusion of such viewpoints encourages the important critical thinking skill of objectively evaluating an author's credentials and bias. This evaluation will illuminate an author's reasons for taking a particular stance on an issue and will aid in readers' evaluation of the author's ideas.

It is our hope that these books will give readers a deeper understanding of the issues debated and an appreciation of the complexity of even seemingly simple issues when good and honest people disagree. This awareness is particularly important in a democratic society such as ours in which people enter into public debate to determine the common good. Those with whom one disagrees should not be regarded as enemies but rather as people whose views deserve careful examination and may shed light on one's own.

Thomas Jefferson once said that "difference of opinion leads to inquiry, and inquiry to truth." Jefferson, a broadly educated man, argued that "if a nation expects to be ignorant and free . . . it expects what never was and never will be." As individuals and as a nation, it is imperative that we consider the opinions of others and examine them with skill and discernment. The Opposing Viewpoints Series is intended to help readers achieve this goal.

David L. Bender and Bruno Leone,
Founders

Greenhaven Press anthologies primarily consist of previously published material taken from a variety of sources, including periodicals, books, scholarly journals, newspapers, government documents, and position papers from private and public organizations. These original sources are often edited for length and to ensure their accessibility for a young adult audience. The anthology editors also change the original titles of these works in order to clearly present the main thesis of each viewpoint and to explicitly indicate the opinion presented in the viewpoint. These alterations are made in consideration of both the reading and comprehension levels of a young adult audience. Every effort is made to ensure that Greenhaven Press accurately reflects the original intent of the authors included in this anthology.

Introduction

"It is impossible to make sense of the special privileges allocated to the press in our society . . . except on the assumption that the press is supposed to serve some important public good."

—*Judith Lichtenberg, philosophy professor and media critic*

The media industry has unique qualities that distinguish it from other industries. One is its privileged legal position under the First Amendment guarantee of freedom of the press, making the media exempt from government restraints and oversight as compared with other businesses. "Why is the press exempt from restraints and restrictions that fall on others?" asks philosophy professor and media critic Judith Lichtenberg. She answers: "Because we believe that the information journalists provide contributes to the search for truth, to democratic citizenship, and to the solution of social problems." The industry's unique legal position carries with it the special responsibility, Lichtenberg and others believe, to give American citizens the information they need to cast informed votes at elections and perform other civic functions in a democratic society.

Many critics have expressed dissatisfaction with how the mass media industry has lived up to such responsibility. Media coverage of political elections has been criticized for focusing on campaign tactics and personal foibles of political candidates rather than substantive issues. Newspapers and television news media programs have been criticized for simply covering the latest murder or sensational crime story rather than substantively investigating the causes of and solutions to crime. Public opinion polls have shown many Americans dissatisfied with news coverage, with complaints ranging from biased reporting to too much of an emphasis on bad news. As a result, writes media critic and author Jay Rosen, "the public today is less and less engaged—in politics and in journalism. The loss of readers and viewers is one result, but the deeper loss is to citizens themselves. People don't see what they care about reflected in the polarized debates and predictable maneuverings of the political class. So they withdraw." One solution to these problems is public journalism.

In public or civic journalism, the media industry makes a more conscious effort to actively engage the public in covering stories of community concern and to search for and promote solutions to social problems. The civic journalism movement has been helped in part by philanthropic organizations such as the Pew Center for Civic Journalism, which between 1993 and 2003 helped fund 120 projects run by newspapers and broadcast stations around the country. In Charlotte, North Carolina, for example, the *Charlotte Observer*, partnering with one television and two radio stations, sought to go beyond simply reporting about crimes, arrests, and trials. Reporters canvassed high-crime neighborhoods and talked with residents to create a series of stories about the causes of crime and neighborhood solutions in its two-year "Taking Back Our Neighborhoods Project." A "community coordinator" who worked for the *Charlotte Observer* (but who was not a reporter) organized neighborhood advisory panels and meetings. In addition to the stories, the newspaper published a "needs" list suggested by Charlotte residents (with items such as baseball gloves to a new recreation center) and a telephone number for volunteers. The project was credited with attracting thousands of dollars in donations and hundreds of citizen volunteers; crime dropped in many of those neighborhoods. The Charlotte story is a good example of how civic journalism has been positive for both the media and for the public, argues Jan Schaffer, former executive director of the Pew Center. "Eight years later, people in those neighborhoods still credit that project with incredible transformations. . . . The paper did not tell people what to do. It just gave a menu of options and people took it from there."

However, the civic journalism movement has come under criticism by some members of the media, who maintain that the public good that the media provides to a community comes solely from its role as an impartial reporter of news. Jane R. Eisner, editorial page editor of the *Philadelphia Inquirer*, argues that trying to stimulate public debates and community activism is not journalism's purpose. She says, "Our central mission is to report the news, to set priorities, to analyze but not to shape or direct events or outcomes. Subsume or diminish this central mission, and we become like any other player in society, like any other politician, interest group, do-gooder, thief. I am not willing to relinquish this unique role." Max Frankel, former *New York Times* editor, has expressed the concern that civic journalism projects such as Charlotte's may drain resources for basic news gathering. He claims that media companies might even avoid coverage of social ills and controversial subjects to avoid alienating their customers. "The best reason for rejecting public journalism, perhaps, is that its rhetoric makes excellent cover for pandering . . . [and] to steer clear of hard-hitting reporting on subjects that the reader is reluctant to hear about."

The debate over the civic journalism movement is fundamentally one over the future direction of America's media and its role in society. It is one of many debates that are examined in *Opposing Viewpoints: Mass Media*. In this volume journalists, media critics, and others provide clashing views on a variety of topics in the following chapters: Is Bias in the Media a Serious Problem? Is Concentration of Media Ownership a Serious Problem? How Do the Media Affect Society? How Will the Media Be Affected by the Internet? The viewpoints highlight the important place the mass media industry continues to occupy in American society and examine the responsibilities of those employed in the industry.

CHAPTER 1

Is Bias in the Media a Serious Problem?

Chapter Preface

Many people believe that the credibility of the mass media is shrinking. In July 1985, 55 percent of the American people believed that journalists "usually get the facts straight," according to a study by the Pew Research Center for the People and the Press. By 2001, according to the organization, that number had dropped to 35 percent. A contributing factor to this decline is the belief held by many Americans that the media have let ideological and political biases distort their presentation of the news. A 1998 Gallup poll revealed that 46 percent of Americans believed the news media—especially network television—have a political bias. (The poll revealed a split in what kind of bias, with 27 percent of those polled saying the media had a liberal bias and 19 percent charging that the media had a conservative bias.)

Conservative media critics often point out that several studies support their contention that people who work in mass media are generally more liberal than other Americans. A 1981 study by the Center for Media and Public Affairs showed that 54 percent of elite journalists (those working for national newspapers, magazines, and television networks) identified themselves as liberal while only 19 percent called themselves conservative. More recently, a 1996 study of Washington, D.C., area journalists showed that self-identified liberals outnumbered conservatives by 61 percent to 9 percent (and that most voted for Democrat Bill Clinton over Republican George H.W. Bush in the 1992 presidential election).

The question of whether the personal political beliefs of those in the media end up contributing to bias in the journalism they produce is the subject of heated debate. ABC news anchor Peter Jennings asserts that journalists strive to prevent their personal beliefs from affecting their objectivity in reporting the news. "One of the good things about journalists is that they recognize bias and work hard to keep it out of their coverage. . . . You can have all sorts of people who voted for Bill Clinton, but the media gave Clinton one hell of a time." However, others contend that personal beliefs inevitably color perceptions, and claims made by liberal journalists that they report the news without bias are not genuine.

These critics argue that outspoken conservatives such as talk radio host Rush Limbaugh are at least honest in presenting themselves as partisan rather than "objective." Thomas Sowell, a conservative columnist and economist, argues that "anyone listening to Rush Limbaugh knows that what he is saying is his own opinion. But people who listen to the news on ABC, CBS or NBC may imagine that they are getting the facts, not just those facts which fit the ideology of the media." The viewpoints in this chapter examine the question of whether and how the media are biased, and how bias may affect how people receive news and information.

"They [the media] slant the news according to their ideologies and find sources who will back them up."

Media Bias Is a Serious Problem

Sheila Gribben Liaugminas

Sheila Gribben Liaugminas has worked in both print and broadcast journalism, including a twenty-year stint as a reporter for *Time* magazine. She is on the editorial board of *Voices*, a publication of Women for Faith & Family, a Roman Catholic women's organization. In the following viewpoint she argues that many members of the news media do not share mainstream American values. She claims that their collective liberal bias has resulted in slanted news coverage and the manipulation of public opinion. Americans must be especially careful and vigilant in separating truth from media spin, she concludes.

As you read, consider the following questions:

1. What arguments by journalist Walter Lippman does Liaugminas believe have special relevance today?
2. What are some of the past experiences the author describes to illustrate her arguments about media bias?
3. What frustration does Liaugminas express about how journalists find expert opinions and quotations to back up their stories?

Sheila Gribben Liaugminas, "How the Media Twists the News," *Crisis*, October 2002, pp. 14–18. Copyright © 2002 by *Crisis*. Reproduced by permission.

In a most ordinary moment on a normal day at work in the Chicago bureau of a major national newsmagazine, I came to a realization that has bothered me ever since. Everyone knows how much power the press has in shaping the news, how its choice of stories and words influence readers. But one afternoon, talking about a rather silly feature story we were doing on pop culture, someone joked, "You know, we can start a trend just by calling it a trend!"

I stopped dead. It was true. But I was the only one not laughing.

Of course, this was hardly an original insight. Walter Lippman—journalist, military intelligence specialist during World War I, propagandist, political scientist, author, and adviser to the presidents—made the same observation a generation ago. These words from his book, *Public Opinion*, bear repeating:

Every newspaper when it reaches the reader is the result of a whole series of selections. . . . In order that [the reader] shall enter he must find a familiar foothold in the story, and this is supplied to him by the use of stereotypes. They tell him that if an association of plumbers is called a "combine" it is appropriate to develop his hostility; if it is called a "group of leading businessmen" the cue is for a favorable reaction. It is in a combination of these elements that the power to create opinion resides.

Why is it so easy to lead people into new behaviors, desires, and attitudes? Why don't people think more critically and see through some of the airy media stories that have no real substance—the stories that are less news than public relations or marketing? As Lippman noted, it's the result of "apathy, preference for the curious trivial as against the dull important, and the hunger for sideshows and three-legged calves."

These days, sideshows and curious trivia have actually gained even greater importance in an industry that has become a confusing mix of news and entertainment. Still, there are people who would like to pay attention to the more consequential events and issues that used to be called news. These can be hard to discern when politics itself has become trivialized. Hence the need to become intelligent news consumers: to learn how to pick through massive fields of information for substantive and fair reporting.

This is a tall task. The manipulation of public opinion is of great importance to both the government and the media. And it takes on added urgency in the months before an election.

Shaping the News

Last year [2001], veteran CBS newsman Bernard Goldberg shocked the media world with his book, *Bias: A CBS Insider Exposes How the Media Distort the News.* He minced no words in laying out the fundamental problem. "The old argument that the networks and other 'media elites' have a liberal bias is so blatantly true that it's hardly worth discussing anymore," he writes. "No, we don't sit around in dark corners and plan strategies on how we're going to slant the news. We don't have to. It comes naturally to most reporters. . . . When you get right down to it, liberals in the newsroom see liberal views as just plain . . . sensible, reasonable, rational views, *which just happen to coincide with their own*" (emphasis added).

Consider this exchange from [Cable News Network] CNN's *American Morning* show. The panelists are talking about the quality of the reporting from the Middle East. Anderson Cooper says, "On both sides of this issue, people see this so clearly one way or the other. It's really fascinating." Paula Zahn: "And it clearly colors their reaction to reporting, and I think it's, you know, very difficult for people to separate their own personal views from the way they interpret the news." Jack Cafferty: "The news media is [sic] only objective if they report something you agree with." Zahn: "Right." Cafferty concludes: "Then they're objective. Otherwise they're biased if you don't agree, you know."

For these three CNN personalities, the news media themselves are impervious to the predispositions and prejudice that afflict their audience. But contrary to what CNN might have us believe, bias is a real problem. You can see it in all the ways the media interpret, frame, and produce the great issues of our day. They slant the news according to their ideologies and find sources who will back them up. Over my 23 years with a newsmagazine, it often did a good—sometimes *very* good—job of reporting and analyzing news and its impact. But sometimes it didn't. Sometimes the editors assigned reporters to a story that had been preconceived in the New

York headquarters—a story with a foregone conclusion.

It was the job of the local bureaus to find people who would give us colorful quotes that fit the theory the story would propose. For instance, the New York office once sent to the bureaus an assignment to do a story on experimental and unproven procedures that "cavalier surgeons" were "getting away with" in the operating room. The story concept assumed the worst—that unchecked surgeons were doing all sorts of impromptu experiments with untested medical instruments in order to pioneer a new operation. Unfortunately, the agenda-driven piece only worked by making invalid comparisons, giving inaccurate medical descriptions, and adding misleading explanations.

Filtering the News

One of the incredible feats of media journalists is denying that there is media bias by equating it with conspiracy theories. *When people share the same bias, they don't need a conspiracy.* The harm comes from the fact that most of the public gets to see only that part of reality which has been filtered through the same preconceptions shared by 90 percent of those in the media.

Thomas Sowell, *Capitalism Magazine*, December 2, 2002.

We at the local bureau had our job cut out for us: to find examples to buttress New York's faulty premise. We were to hunt down quotes about surgeons who have too much freedom in trying out risky new techniques.

In other words, the magazine had decided there was a controversy and then had to scramble to find evidence to prove it. It was clearly off the mark, and so I reported at length on what I found, with strong quotes from strong sources (including the vice president of the Society of Thoracic Surgeons). The experts I interviewed explained with great clarity the very complicated process of advanced life-saving surgery—both its risks and its benefits. (The vice president had said: "It's mind-boggling how low the failure rate is, so we're kind of looking around and wondering why people aren't standing up and cheering and saying, 'You guys are doing a hell of a job!'" Predictably, that quote never got used.)

Happily, the article that appeared in the magazine was substantially different from the tone and original intent of the assignment. Score one for truth. But I can't say that was always the result. Often, if the reporting didn't fit the required conclusions and desired slant of the piece, it just didn't make it into the story at all.

"In the higher bureaucracy organizations—the major media—editors pay less attention because they're busy doing other things," observes Chicago writer and media raconteur Gary Ruderman, a former colleague who left the magazine several years before I did. "They choose not to be informed, and they don't do the work to find out the truth behind the rumors and hearsay."

Or as Goldberg puts it, "National TV reporters, as a group, are lazy.". . .

Veteran newsman Jim Hatfield was an exception to the rule, referring to himself as a "Genghis Khan" in the newsroom. He went from newsman for KPIX in the late 1960s to news writer for KNBC, to executive producer for KABC in Hollywood, and then to the CBS-owned station WBBM in Chicago as news director, producer, and executive producer of magazine programming. "It's more difficult now to get an accurate picture from the news media," notes Hatfield, who does freelance work from his home outside Chicago. "The broad spectrum of media now, especially with the advent of the Internet, has added pressure and forced changes in the broadcast arena. They've hired younger, less experienced people and have pushed for the most sensational angles possible. The levels of taste and sensitivity that we always observed, the lines we would never cross, are just about gone now."

"The problem comes in the big social and cultural issues, where we often sound more like flacks for liberal causes than objective journalists," Goldberg admits. "It's a world where money is often seen as a solution to social problems, where antiabortionists are seen as kooks and weirdos." The major network chiefs take their cues every day from the *New York Times*, he says, and all reporting derives from that worldview. "It's scary to think that so many important people who bring Americans the news can be so delusional." Scary because, as Goldberg notes, "It's not just that so many journalists are so different from mainstream America. It's that some are downright hostile to what many Americans hold sacred." And these are the creators of American public opinion. . . .

Stopping the Spin

In a world of media spin, it's not easy to keep one's own balance. First, know what your core values are, what you hold to be objectively true. Be discriminating in your selection of news sources and carefully scrutinize everything you hear and read—see how it resonates with what you believe.

Note how news gatherers select subjects and how they cover them. What photographs do they choose? Do their accounts sound slanted, or do they present compelling voices from both sides of an issue?

Notice their sources: Do you hear from the same set of "experts" again and again? I find this especially annoying. The newsmagazine I worked for is still using some of the same old liberal "news analysts" they used when I first arrived in the Midwest bureau more than two decades ago. And you see them all over television news as well. When the topic is Catholicism, the networks all call on the same dissident priests and ex-priests, feminists, and "Catholics for a Free Choice": Andrew Greeley, Eugene Kennedy, Charles Curran, Richard Sipe, Frances Kissling, and so on. Paula Zahn has continually used Sipe as the go-to expert on the troubles within the Church, always describing him as a "retired priest." He's an ex-priest, Paula. There's a difference.

"They don't want our new, fresh sources when they've got the regulars who give them the quotes they want," Ruderman says, sharing my observation that the major media, like the newsmagazine we worked for, have all taken the easy route of using dog-eared Rolodexes to call on the same talking heads. "They never wanted my sources when they didn't fit the mold of what they wanted the story to say. They had a preconceived idea of the status quo, and so they would always go to the status-quo sources for their standard comments.". . .

Democracy and the Press

It's interesting how much of Lippman's analysis from 70 years ago still applies to the media. In the foreword to the 1997 edition of *Public Opinion*, Ronald Steel recalls that from a young age, Lippman studied politics and the press. "In *Liberty and the News* he concluded that the newspaper stories of one of the seminal events of the century (the Russian Revolution) were distorted and inaccurate, based not on the facts but on the 'hopes of the men who composed the news organization.'"

Lippman then posed a more fundamental problem, as Steel relates: "How could the public get the information it needed to make rational political judgments if it could not rely on the press? Unbiased information had become essential, he argued, because 'decisions in a modern state tend to be made by the interaction, not of Congress and the executive, but of public opinion and the executive.'. . . For this reason the accuracy of news reporting, the protection of the sources of public opinion, had become the 'basic problem of democracy.'"

The power of public opinion, which is supposed to be the driving force behind most important decisions in a democracy, can itself be driven or steered by the prejudices of unofficial opinion-makers. Vigilance and self-awareness are its only protection. Which is why, wherever they get their news, intelligent citizens will take nothing for granted except their principles.

"Media bias may not be as harmful as many people think."

Media Bias Is Not a Serious Problem

Tyler Cohen

Both left-wing and right-wing critics who complain about media bias are mistaken, writes economist Tyler Cohen in the following viewpoint. What may seem like political or ideological bias is in reality the result of the media striving to attract an audience by providing compelling and marketable stories. Media bias should not be considered an overly serious problem, Cohen concludes, because the media are limited in their power to influence what people think; most people recognize that the media are often biased and are thus able to draw their own conclusions about issues and stories. Cohen is a professor of economics at George Mason University in Virginia.

As you read, consider the following questions:
1. How and why did media coverage of the 2003 Iraq war change, according to Cohen?
2. Why are the media obsessed with crime and personal scandals, according to the author?
3. Why does Cohen consider the media to be a sideshow?

Both left-wing and right-wing commentators lament media bias. The right wing cites the predominant Democratic orientations—often 80 to 90 percent—of major journalists. The left wing cites the right wing pundits, such as Rush Limbaugh, or the growing success of Fox News. Why do the major media sometimes slant to the left, and other times slant to the right? The answer is simple: viewers want them to. We look to the media for entertainment, drama, and titillation before objectivity. Journalists, to get ahead, must produce marketable stories with some kind of emotional slant, which typically will have broader political implications. The result: it looks like media bias when in fact journalists, operating in a highly competitive environment, are simply doing their best to attract an audience.

War and Scandals

Consider the [2003] war with Iraq. Leading up to the war, and during the fighting, CNN and other American media treated the Bush regime with kid gloves. We saw little of the civilian casualties that filled news screens around the world. Yet after the war the American media appear to be far more critical of the Bush plans. Almost every day [in late 2003] we hear about suicide bomb attacks, and until lately we have had little exposure to rebuilding progress in Iraq.

What happened? Has the media changed its collective mind about our foreign policy? Maybe, but a simpler explanation operates. In each case the media chose the presentation that made for the best story. "Heroic American fighters" was the best and most marketable story before and during the major fighting. "Suicide bomber attacks" has proven to be a forceful story in the last few months. "American soldiers rebuilding schools" doesn't draw as big a crowd. In fact recently the pro-war side has done better by pushing "outrage that war critics neglect progress in Iraq" as a slant.

The media appear obsessed with personal scandals, such as the victims of toxic waste dumps, or women whose breast implants have poisoned their bodies. . . . The media thus appear to be hard on corporations, sympathetic to government regulation, and, as a result, "left-wing." But again, they are looking for a good and marketable story, and yes this includes Monica Lewinsky.[1] Journalists are seeking to advance their careers more than a political agenda.

For purposes of contrast, look at crime. Crime, and crime victims, make among the most compelling stories. Remember the obsession with the [Washington] DC area sniper case? Not surprisingly, people who watch TV receive the impression that crime is very high, if only because they see so much crime on TV. The contrasting reality is that most people in America lead very safe lives. Nonetheless the "left-wing" media appear to take a "right-wing" stance when it comes to warning us about crime, again in search of a better story.

The Media's Dirty Little Secret

Today's conservatives scoff at the professed objectivity of network news reporters and newspaper correspondents, often brandishing a 1995 survey by the Roper Center and Freedom Forum as their smoking gun. The survey showed that 89% of the journalists polled voted for Bill Clinton in 1992, while only 7% cast a ballot for George Bush. One problem with conservative interpretations of this study is that they assume that politics trumps professionalism for liberal journalists but not for conservative ones. Far more likely is that, for both liberal and conservative journalists, politics has roughly the same priority it has for any of us regardless of profession. When there is bias, and it does exist, one can chalk it up to the personal rather than the political, or to the press' herd instinct for ganging up as long as doing so fits the public temper at the time.

The dirty little secret of network newscasts, and of most major newspapers, is not that they are manned by liberal proselytizers. It is that they are trying to attract the widest possible viewership, or readership, and that doing so necessitates that they be as inoffensive as possible. That is why investigative reports seem so toothless, gumming away at government boondoggles or consumer fraud or corrupt politicians that are unlikely to infuriate either the left or the right.

Neal Gabler, *Los Angeles Times*, December 22, 2002.

Media favor coverage that can be packaged. The OJ trial,[2] for instance, had dramatic developments with some frequency,

---

1. the intern whose affair with President Bill Clinton helped lead to Clinton's impeachment   2. O.J. Simpson, a famous retired football star and a movie actor, was tried and eventually acquitted of killing his wife and another person in 1994.

regular characters, and a fairly simple plot line. It resembled a daily soap opera, and not surprisingly it was immensely popular on TV. For similar reasons, serial killers will receive attention disproportionate to their number of victims.

Some economic points have an especially hard time getting a fair shake from the media. It is easy to show how a government program put Joe Smith back to work. Arguably the expenditure was a waste, once we consider the "hidden costs of opportunities foregone," but this abstract concept does not make for an easy visual, much less a good interview. In similar fashion, the media do little to show the benefits of free trade.

Using the Media

In sum, media bias may not be as harmful as many people think. It is perhaps sad that we do not look much to the news for objective information, but this same fact limits the damage that slanted coverage can cause. Keep in mind that many *definitions* of media bias mean that the media think one way, and the citizenry thinks another way. So clearly the media have not succeeded in forcing us all into the same mold.

We should resist the temptation to think that the TV screen, or the newspaper Op-Ed page, or the blogosphere for that matter, is the critical arena deciding the fate of the world. In reality, these media are a sideshow to the more general human preoccupation with stories. We use TV and other media to suit our personal purposes, not vice versa. No, the media are not fair, but they are unfair in ways different than you might imagine. They are unfair because you, collectively, as viewers, want them to be unfair.

"What it adds up to is a media heavily biased toward conservative politics and conservative politicians."

Liberal Media Bias Is a Myth

E.J. Dionne

E.J. Dionne is a columnist for the *Washington Post* and a senior fellow at the Brookings Institution. His books include *Why Americans Hate Politics* and *They Only Look Dead: Why Progressives Will Dominate the Next Political Era*. In the following viewpoint he refutes the argument that the media are dominated by and are biased in favor of liberals. He contends that newspaper editors and television network executives are highly sensitive to conservative complaints about bias, and that conservatives now dominate such media outlets as cable television and talk radio. As a result, mass media in the United States has become biased in favor of conservative politics and politicians, he concludes.

As you read, consider the following questions:
1. How does Dionne describe the conventional wisdom regarding media bias?
2. The media have preferred the values of which class of people, according to the author?
3. What are the traditional news sources, according to Dionne?

The fat is in the fire on the issue of media bias, and that is a good thing. It's time to revisit a matter on which the conventional wisdom is, roughly, 180 degrees off.

You hear the conventional wisdom all the time from shrewd conservative commentators who understand that political pressure, relentlessly applied, usually achieves its purposes. They have sold the view that the media are dominated by liberals and that the news is skewed against conservatives.

This belief fueled the construction of a large network of conservative institutions—especially on radio and cable television—that provides conservative viewpoints close to 24 hours a day. Conservatives argued that hopelessly left-wing establishment news sources needed to be balanced by brave, relentless voices from the right.

But the continuing attacks on mainstream journalists have another effect. Because the drumbeat of conservative press criticism has been so steady, the establishment press has internalized it. Editors and network executives are far more likely to hear complaints from the right than from the left.

A Shift to the Right

To the extent that there has been a bias in the establishment media, it has been less a liberal tilt than a preference for the values of the educated, professional class—which, surprise, surprise, is roughly the class position of most journalists.

This meant that on social and cultural issues—abortion and religion come to mind—journalism was not particularly hospitable to conservative voices. But on economic issues—especially free trade and balanced budgets—the press tilted toward the center or even toward moderate conservatism. You might say that the two groups most likely to be mistreated by the media were religious conservatives and trade unionists.

But even that view is out of date, because the definition of "media" commonly used in judging these matters is faulty. And that's why you are beginning to hear liberals and Democrats make a new argument. Earlier this week [in a December 3, 2002,] speech former president Bill Clinton contrasted what he called an "increasingly right-wing and bellicose conservative press" with "an increasingly docile establishment press." A couple of weeks back [on November 5, 2002], Senate Democratic Leader Tom Daschle lashed out at radio talk show host Rush Limbaugh. He said Limbaugh's attacks were so "shrill" that "the threats against those of us in public life go up dramatically, against us and against our families."

Note the response of the so-called liberal media. Rather than join an outcry against Limbaugh, the establishment commentary was mostly aimed against Daschle and picked up the conservative cry that he was "whining." Limbaugh was invited for lengthy and respectful interviews. . . .

Hernandez. © 1998 by R. Hernandez. Reproduced by permission.

Now, television hosts are free to invite anyone they wish (they've even had me on), and cable networks long for a piece of Limbaugh's large audience. But that is the point: Limbaugh's new respectability is the surest sign that the conservative talk network is now bleeding into what passes for the mainstream media, just as the unapologetic conservatism of the Fox News Channel is now affecting programming on the other cable networks. This shift to the right is occurring as cable becomes a steadily more important source of news.

Continuing Complaints

All this constitutes a genuine triumph for conservatives. But rather than rest on their laurels, they continue to pound away at any media deviation from their version of political correctness. . . .

When Katie Couric had the nerve to ask some tough questions of EPA [Environmental Protection Agency] Administrator Christine Todd Whitman on [an episode of the] "Today" show, the ever-alert conservative Media Research Center trashed Couric for bias. When the *Chicago Tribune* ran an unflattering picture of President [George W.] Bush on its Nov. 14 [2002] front page, it was assailed for a lack of patriotism. Editors who worry about conservative criticism are not paranoid. You just wonder: Where have the liberals been?

It took conservatives a lot of hard and steady work to push the media rightward. It dishonors that work to continue to presume that—except for a few liberal columnists—there is any such thing as the big liberal media. The media world now includes (1) talk radio, (2) cable television and (3) the traditional news sources (newspapers, newsmagazines and the old broadcast networks). Two of these three major institutions tilt well to the right, and the third is under constant pressure to avoid even the pale hint of liberalism. These institutions, in turn, influence the burgeoning world of online news and commentary.

What it adds up to is a media heavily biased toward conservative politics and conservative politicians. Kudos to the right. Now, what will the rest of us do about the new bias?

*"Big Media remains a fortress of
liberalism."*

Liberal Media Bias Is Not a Myth

Pat Buchanan

Pat Buchanan, a former speechwriter and adviser for presidents Richard Nixon, Gerald Ford, and Ronald Reagan, is a nationally syndicated columnist and a founder and editor of the magazine *American Conservative*. He was twice a candidate for the Republican presidential nomination, and ran for president under the Reform Party in 2000. In the viewpoint that follows, he argues that claims that liberal media bias is a myth are unfounded. The media—by which he means the nation's television networks and major newspapers—are demonstrably liberal, both in their editorial positions and in the political leanings of their staffs. While conservative views have gained a foothold in some places—notably talk radio and cable television—"Big Media" remains biased against conservatives, Buchanan concludes.

As you read, consider the following questions:

1. What standard does Buchanan use to measure liberal and conservative?
2. What media figures and institutions does the author identify as being liberal?
3. What distinction does Buchanan make between "Big Media" and "the populist and democratic media?"

"What Liberal Media?" blared the monster headline atop the full-page ad in the *New York Times*. Its author was Eric Alterman of the *Nation*, who has a book out of the same title.

There was a touch of irony in Alterman's choosing the *Times* to place an ad declaring liberal bias to be a "myth." For that paper has lately been embroiled in the greatest scandal in its history, the Jayson Blair affair, caused by almost blind devotion to liberalism's god of "diversity" in the newsroom.[1]

And, as a judge of bias, Alterman is poorly situated. He is so far left he considers network anchors Dan Rather [CBS] and Peter Jennings [ABC] to be conservatives. Moreover, he argues from exceptions to prove his rules. Because the *Times* endorsed [the 2002 reelection of] New York Gov. George Pataki over a hapless black Democratic nominee [Carl McCall], Alterman argues, the *Times* is not really reliably liberal.

If this issue of media bias is to be discussed, there is a need for some standard of left-to-right. Let me suggest a simple one. If [Democrat] Al Gore is center-left and [Republican] George Bush center-right, one measure of whether a publication is liberal or conservative would be whether it endorsed Gore or Bush [in the 2000 presidential election campaign]—and which party's presidential candidate it almost always endorses. And if being pro-life and in favor of Bush's tax cuts is conservative and being pro-choice and against the Bush tax cuts is liberal, what then constitutes the liberal press?

Answer: All three major networks, PBS, NPR and virtually all major U.S. papers—*Boston Globe, New York Times, Philadelphia Inquirer, Baltimore Sun, Washington Post, Atlanta Constitution, Miami Herald, Chicago Tribune, Denver Post, Los Angeles Times*. While the *Wall Street Journal* editorial page is neoconservative, *USA Today*—the nation's largest newspaper—is left of center.

Not only are the editorial pages of most major papers liberal, the news staffs are overwhelmingly so. At the annual White House correspondents dinners, conservatives are a

1. Jayson Blair was a reporter who was fired in May 2003 from the *New York Times* for writing plagiarized and/or fabricated stories. Some commentators suggested that his supervisors failed to dismiss or discipline Blair sooner because he was black.

tiny minority. Opinion surveys of the national press found 80 percent to 90 percent voted for McGovern and Mondale, though Nixon and Reagan both carried 49 states.[2] How many celebrity journalists can you name who support Operation Rescue?[3]

If the network news anchors are liberal, so, too, are the hosts of the morning shows, Matt Lowry, Katie Couric, Diane Sawyer and Charlie Gibson. The anchors of the Sunday interview shows are Tim Russert, off [former Democratic senator] Pat Moynihan's staff, and George Stephanopolous, from [former Democratic president] Bill Clinton's staff, and Bob Schieffer of CBS, whom no one has ever accused of being a Dixiecrat.

A Big Lie

Ultimately, the assertion that today's media are not liberal is a big lie, and one that most American citizens instinctively disagree with. Somehow it doesn't occur to . . . the many . . . reporters in denial that Fox News and Rush Limbaugh are giving Americans something they want very much and feel is missing from other media offerings.

Jonah Goldberg, *American Enterprise*, July/August 2003.

Alterman does, however, have a valid point about commentators. Following [Vice President] Spiro Agnew's attack on the national press in 1969, most major newspapers—realizing they had lost touch with millions of readers—began creating op-ed pages and opening them up to conservatives. Today, columnists on the right are fully competitive and many are more widely syndicated than their liberal colleagues.

After the breakthrough by conservative columnists came the breakthrough in talk radio. Rush Limbaugh, Sean Hannity, Neil Boortz, Ollie North, Gordon Liddy, Michael Savage, Michael Reagan and other conservatives dominate talk radio, nationally and locally. It is hard to name a liberal who has succeeded in national radio.

---

2. George McGovern was the Democratic presidential nominee in 1972; he lost to Richard Nixon. Walter Mondale, the 1984 Democratic nominee, lost to Ronald Reagan.   3. a controversial antiabortion protest group

Among the magazines of politics and opinion, [the conservative] *National Review*, the *Weekly Standard*, *Human Events* and the *American Conservative* have a combined circulation far higher than [the liberal] the *Nation* and the *New Republic*. In cable TV, Fox News, which is now predominant, tilts toward [President George W.] Bush, but CNN, whose anchors are Judy Woodruff, Wolf Blitzer and Aaron Brown, lists heavily to port.

Conclusion: Big Media remains a fortress of liberalism, but in the populist and democratic media—the op-ed pages, the Internet, cable TV, talk radio—where people have a variety of voices from which to choose—conservatives prevail. With this caveat: The House of Conservatism is a house divided. Conservatives of today are not the conservatives of yesterday. . . . They have made their peace with Big Government. . . .

Many of today's conservatives would have been called liberals in the 1960s. Indeed, some were liberals then. And their progeny have come to accept foreign aid, the Department of Education, even the National Endowment for the Arts.

They call it compassionate conservatism.

"What I have learned during more than a decade as a daily journalist is that race matters greatly in newsrooms."

Bias Against Minorities Remains a Problem in the Media

Pamela Newkirk

Pamela Newkirk is a professor of journalism at New York University and the author of *Within the Veil: Black Journalists, White Media*. The following viewpoint is taken from a speech she made for the Center for Integration and Improvement in Journalism, an organization that promotes ethnic diversity in the media. Newkirk argues that the nation's newsrooms remain dominated by whites and that journalists who are members of racial minority groups continue to face bias and discrimination from their colleagues. Such prejudice hampers the ability of news organizations to accurately and objectively report the news and cover the lives of African Americans and other groups. News media organizations should continue to strive for racial and ethnic diversity through their hiring procedures and their media coverage, she concludes.

As you read, consider the following questions:
1. How have the numbers of minority journalists changed in recent years, according to Newkirk?
2. What problems have many minority reporters experienced in dealing with their colleagues, according to the author?
3. What advice does Newkirk have for young people considering journalism as a career?

There are those in prominent places who would say . . . efforts [to promote minority journalists] are no longer needed—that America's newsrooms are diverse enough. And there are some well meaning people who turn on the television news to find black, brown, yellow and red faces, and therefore agree.

But . . . news diversity remains far from real. The [2002] survey released by the American Society of Newspaper Editors show that America's newsrooms are still 88 percent white. The percentage of journalists of color has remained stagnant at roughly 12 percent—this despite the fact that racial minorities comprise more than 30 percent of the national population. Several years ago [in 1998] ASNE acknowledged that its two-decades-long mission for racial parity in the newsroom by the year 2000 had failed.

The good news, however, was that the percentage of minority journalists did not drop in the last survey as it had in the previous one [in 2001] (the actual number of journalitst of color increased by four, from 6,563 to 6,567). But given a period of consistent setbacks, diversity advocates are left to view stagnation as progress.

Musical Chairs

A close reading of the [2002] survey shows that journalists of color continue to leave the industry almost as quickly as they are hired, making diversity even more elusive. While 447 journalists of color were hired this past year [2002], during the same period, 443 left the industry.

A Freedom Forum survey released two years ago [in 2000] showed that while the industry had hired 550 journalists of color each year since 1994, 400 journalists of color have annually left the business. And last year [2001], ASNE figures showed that while 596 journalists of color had been hired, by year's end, 698 had left, resulting in the first decrease in 23 years.

I attribute this game of musical chairs to the ways in which journalists of color are undervalued in the newroom. While those of us who advocate diversity concentrate on numbers, we often ignore the resistance in the newsroom to ideas emanating from the journalists of color who are already there.

The inability to influence coverage in meaningful ways has pushed many journalists of color out of the door. Left behind are newspapers and newscasts that lack complexity or insight.

Diversity Void

And while I have in recent years focused my attention on journalists of color, I have cringed in recent weeks as the gay community has been scapegoated in the Catholic Church scandal [involving priests accused of sexual abuse of children]. Many journalists have used the terms gay and pedophile almost interchangeably, as if the criminal act of violating children is a gay issue. The problem of pedophiles is not one of sexual orientation. They often violate children of both sexes indiscriminately. I can only imagine that this problematic coverage is due to a diversity void.

The diversity void was graphic following 9/11,[1] when many Americans were left without tools to contextualize the anti-American rage that has been building across the globe. We have seen white America react similarly after a festering hopelessness and rage finally exploded in America's inner-cities. If only the media would adequately reflect these diverse strains of thought which would enable us to open avenues of understanding before these cataclysmic eruptions.

While for many of us 9/11 remains beyond comprehension, true diversity in the media could have helped explain why so many blacks celebrated the acquittal of O.J. Simpson,[2] or that the mistrust by many blacks of the criminal justice system is rooted in reason. It's a rational response to a long history of consistently negative experiences. Blacks and whites have separate and not always equal histories and reach different—and equally valid—conclusions. But too often the black perspective is presented as irrational, rather than reasoned.

Childhood Dream Fulfilled

Race still matters, but many point to Colin Powell, Condoleeza Rice[3] and a handful of fortune 500 CEO's and pretend

1. On September 11, 2001, terrorists hijacked planes and used them as bombs in attacks in New York City and Washington, D.C., killing three thousand people. 2. Simpson, a retired football player, was tried and acquitted of murdering his wife in a controversial 1994 trial. 3. Powell and Rice both served as senior administration officials under President George W. Bush.

it doesn't. And what I have learned during more than a decade as a daily journalist is that race matters greatly in newsrooms. In 1993 as I ended a daily newspaper career I reflected on a journey that had taken me to four different news organizations and had fulfilled a childhood dream. From the time I was 12 I wanted to be a journalist. I knew of the role the news media had played during the civil rights movement and saw first-hand its role in toppling a corrupt presidency following Watergate.

I wanted to make a difference in how African Americans and other disenfranchised groups were portrayed. At four different newspapers I worked my way up from a suburban reporter outside of Albany, New York to the state capital bureau to Capitol Hill and New York City. I covered many of the prized stories in my respective newsrooms: the 1988 presidential campaign and that year's Democratic National Convention; two presidential inaugurations; a mayoral race which resulted in the election of New York's first black mayor; and in 1990, from South Africa, I witnessed the release from prison of Nelson Mandela and the dismantling of apartheid.

And in 1992 I was among the New York *Newsday* reporters to share a Pulitzer Prize for spot news for our coverage of a fatal subway crash.

Swimming Against the Tide

But despite my success, it was debatable whether I and the legions of other African American reporters I had known had made an appreciable difference in the way African Americans and other people of color were portrayed.

What could be said if one was to judge us by the preponderance of stereotypes that routinely fill television newscasts and newspapers?

In the newsroom I often found myself swimming against the tide. Many of my ideas were viewed with suspicion or alarm. I often encountered stiff resistance to ideas my editors viewed as alien. A fixed and warped view of black life made my efforts to present balanced portraits of African Americans and others who fell out of the mainstream nearly impossible. Many story ideas emanating from communities deemed unimportant were dismissed. Black elected officials and community leaders who lacked the flamboyance of the Rev. Al Sharpton were ignored. I had, to be sure, won some newsroom battles, but the war for fair and balanced coverage raged on.

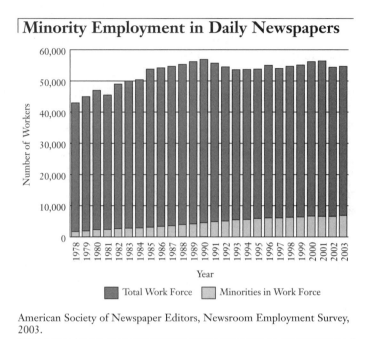

Minority Employment in Daily Newspapers

American Society of Newspaper Editors, Newsroom Employment Survey, 2003.

In 1993 I joined the journalism faculty at New York University. In my new realm I had the luxury of time to reflect on my career and on the careers of thousands of African American journalists who had joined mainstream news organizations. I expected to focus on the decades since the national advisory commission on civil disorders fixed the spotlight on news media bias in reporting and hiring. But what I found was a much longer and protracted struggle by African Americans to diversify the mainstream media.

Footnotes in History

Left out of, or reduced to footnotes in media history books was the razor sharp critique of the media by journalists like Lester Walton and John Bruce early in the 20th century; the daring reportage of the *New York Post*'s Ted Poston who risked injury and death to expose racial injustice in the south; the insightful analysis of Earl Brown for *Life* magazine in the 1940s and the sometimes painful quest by legions of black journalists to broaden the scope on black life.

Left in the archives or stored in the memory banks of veterans are stories of journalists who, from the moment they set foot in white dominated newsrooms, have had to swim against the tide.

In interviews conducted around the country many black journalists told me that they feel pressured to validate a societal perception of black pathology in order to succeed in their newsrooms. And they feel their credibility assaulted or harshly scrutinized when they attempt to present balanced portraits of black life.

If one doubts that rewards are great for those who fuel perceptions of black pathology, one only has to consider the quick rise of Janet Cooke after she wrote "Jimmy's World" for the *Washington Post*. Her story was of an 8-year-old heroin addict who shot drugs in his mother's drug den. Not only did the story make the cover of the paper, but it quickly earned Cooke a promotion from the paper's district weekly section. Cooke became the darling of the newspaper.

The story, of course, was found to have been a complete fabrication, but only after it was awarded a Pulitzer Prize. And even the Pulitzer underscored how portraits of black pathology are rewarded. Cooke simply concocted a tale that she knew would bring her acclaim.

Loyalty Questioned

Meanwhile, the loyalty of African American journalists was questioned in and outside the industry. Many say while their editors expect them to focus on the underside of black life to "prove" their objectivity, many of their black brethren view them as traitors who are all too willing to sell out black people for career advancement.

Centuries of demeaning stereotypes in the nation's leading publications have instilled in many blacks a deep mistrust of the mainstream news media that only decades of fair and balanced portrayals can hope to undo.

To make matters worse, many African American journalists are constantly told that 'they' are at an advantage, even as they hold only five percent of newspaper jobs nationally. Many news executives have fueled racial animosity by telling white candidates that specific jobs were being reserved for journalists of color, stoking the false perception of a minority advantage.

During the centuries that newsrooms were exclusively staffed by whites, few if any of them were told their jobs were due to their race, even as they all happened to be white.

Perspectives Squashed

Certainly there is much to be gained by hiring people whose backgrounds, cultural experiences and ideas tap into untapped reservoirs of important stories. This would make for a more dynamic and reflective newsroom—one where the blind spots of individual journalists could be illuminated by a sometimes noisy orchestra of diverse journalists. But instead diverse perspectives are too often squashed in the newsroom. Many journalists of color report that their contributions to stories like the O.J. Simpson trial or the [1992] Los Angeles riots were undervalued or ignored because they challenged status quo assumptions about African Americans.

Many are angry daily over a racial pecking order that places greatest importance to white victims of crime. This resistance to diverse thought has resulted in disillusionment, anger, and ultimately, the exodus of many.

In recent years many groups have pledged millions of dollars to diversity efforts. The Freedom Forum has committed $5 million to media diversity initiatives. The Scripps Howard Foundation is spending $7 million to build a journalism school at the historically black Hampton University. The Ford Foundation has directed $1 million to a news diversity program at Columbia University. Like in the 1960s, huge sums of money is being devoted to news diversity. But none of these efforts will bear fruit unless news executives begin to value the diversity already in their midst.

An Economic Imperative

Finally, when speaking in these venues, I am often urged to offer signs of hope—as if painting a rosy picture of the news industry can make it so. I can say that in 34 years we have gone from newsrooms that were virtually all white to those where diversity is, if not a reality, an expectation. And I can say that if news organizations are to survive, the nation's rapidly changing racial demographics make more fair and balanced coverage an economic imperative.

And to the young people here who choose to enter this field, I will tell you that few vocations can match the opportunity journalism presents to exercise your ideals. For despite the many challenges you'll face, journalism is—at its height—a noble profession. On the days that you are allowed to make a difference, to contribute to meaningful discourse in our communities, you will have performed an invaluable public service. Unlike many of your peers, you will do work with meaning that goes far beyond a fat paycheck. Journalism is an evangelical calling, particularly when you use it as a light to make the world a better place.

I advise you to learn about great journalists—like Frederick Douglass, Ida B. Wells and Bob Maynard—and use their life's work as a beacon. And hopefully one day you will be in a position to pass on a torch that many illustrious people have played a part in lighting. All the best to you. Onward and upward!

"Instead of making public discourse more intellectually sophisticated, the journalistic propaganda on diversity has helped dumb it down."

Efforts to Fight Media Bias Against Minorities Are Misguided

William McGowan

William McGowan argues in the following viewpoint that efforts by newspapers and other media organizations to promote affirmative action and racial and ethnic diversity have been made at the expense of traditional journalistic values such as honesty and objectivity. The media have become overly sensitive on the issue of race and now treat certain minority groups such as homosexuals preferentially, he contends. In consequence, there has been a decline in public trust of the media and a failure by the media to adequately cover certain controversial topics, such as black-on-black crime. McGowan, a former reporter for *Newsweek* and the British Broadcasting Corporation (BBC), is the author of the book *Coloring the News: How Crusading for Diversity Has Corrupted American Journalism.*

As you read, consider the following questions:

1. What news story did the editors of the *Philadelphia Daily News* feel compelled to apologize for, according to McGowan?
2. What are some of the unintended consequences of the media's crusade for diversity, in McGowan's opinion?

William McGowan, "Undone by Diversity Bias," *The World & I*, March 2003, pp. 64–69. Copyright © 2003 by News World Communications, Inc. Reproduced by permission.

In August 2002, the *Philadelphia Daily News* ran a cover story about the number of fugitives who were wanted on murder charges. There were 41 blacks, 12 Hispanics, and 3 Asians with warrants out on them. No whites in Philadelphia were being sought at the time.

In typical tabloid fashion, the *Daily News'* cover featured mug shots of some of the suspects—15 pictures in all. Editors at the paper took pains to ensure that these photos were racially and ethnically "representative." But the preponderance of black faces sparked a furor, with a threatened protest march and boycott.

A Controversial Apology

In a signed apology, *Daily News* Managing Editor Ellen Foley said she was sorry if the graphic treatment offended black Philadelphians. "The front-page photos from last Thursday sent the message to some readers that only black men commit murder. That was a mistake," she wrote. The paper would surely do a story on fugitive murderers again, Foley insisted, but would do it differently though she didn't specify how. In an interview, she maintained that any future efforts would not prompt readers to think "that all killers are black and that all black men are killers."

Calling the apology "bunk," radio talk show host and weekly *News* columnist Michael Smerconish pointed out that murder in Philadelphia is in fact an overwhelmingly black thing. Whites represent over half of the city's population but only 5 percent of its murderers, while African Americans make up less than half the population but represent over three-quarters of its alleged killers. In addition, he pointed out, virtually all alleged murderers were the same race as their victims, with over 90 percent of black victims dying at the hands of another African American.

"Instead of discussing why black-on-black crime threatens the city—minorities in particular—we're caught up in a bogus debate as to whether the paper should have presented the information the way it did," Smerconish charged. It was not the *Daily News'* fault that 56 nonwhites were being sought for murder, he said, "but in the twisted racial world in which we live, this is perceived to be the fault of the newspaper."

Supporters of efforts to enhance diversity in the main-stream media say news organizations need to hire and promote minority journalists so they can better reflect the communities they serve. Diversity supporters also say that the news media should do a better job of identifying and affirming "distinct and unique" minority points of view; journalists should be more sensitive in reporting and commenting on issues involving minority communities. But as racial and ethnic controversies at scores of news organizations around the country in the last decade or so suggest, this diversity crusade may have run off the rails. Sensitivity is fine. Yet what we are seeing more and more, critics say, is hypersensitivity and political correctness, as journalistic candor and honesty take a backseat to a narrow orthodoxy on vexing diversity-related issues of race, homosexual rights, immigration, and affirmative action.

Racial Conflict

On race, for example, the pro-diversity journalistic script downplays the value and accomplishments of integration and encourages the kind of cultural relativism and double standards that make it hard to explore the more troubling realities of underclass dysfunction in this country with the candor and completeness required. Additionally, the script on race tends to mute the reporting on unflattering incidents of black racism and black anti-Semitism, minimizing or ignoring the very troubling reality that blacks are many times more likely to commit violent crimes against whites than the reverse.

In 1997, in one of the more brutal incidents of interracial violence in this country, three white teenagers from rural Michigan ended up in a black neighborhood in Flint, Michigan, and were set upon by a gang of black youths. One of the boys was shot to death, and the girl in the group was raped. A minor, one-day news story, this attack achieved little national prominence and quickly disappeared.

A year before, in 1996, though, when it appeared that U.S. Army Special Forces at Fort Bragg might be painting swastikas on the doors of black soldiers' rooms, the story grabbed banner headlines and received broad network attention. The story faded only when it was revealed that the culprit was a black soldier.

The journalistic script on race also tends to see racism everywhere. This has at points encouraged the press to rush off and cry wolf where facts don't merit it, play into the hands of racial arsonists with agendas, and deny the facts of blacks' progress to justify the continuation of racial preferences.

A Bias Template

Bias is real and ought to be reported when found, but the prevalence of the unchecked bias report is another matter. Part of the problem is that storytelling about bias, as columnist Michael Kelly points out, is a standard "template" in the modern newsroom culture. Journalists tend to feel that bigotry is widespread in America and they are primed to see it quickly when their counterparts in the lobbying world send in their reports. This explains why stories about alleged racial slurs among Texaco executives and the wave of church burnings in the South were still being framed as bias news long after the evidence showed that this framing was wrong. This media tilt has the effect of discounting the real gains of out-groups and depicting the country as much more prejudiced than it really is. And it has effects on news consumers in general. It's one reason why so few people trust the press.

John Leo, *U.S. News & World Report*, November 22, 1999.

Although the facts behind the 1996 wave of arson attacks on black churches in the South were complicated, news organizations were quick to declare that Mississippi was burning once again. A nationwide conspiracy of racist whites, buoyed by a growing backlash against affirmative action, supposedly stood behind the flames. When contradictory facts emerged in isolated corrective reporting, newspapers, TV, and newsmagazines largely ignored them, leaving the impression that hate was the only root.

A Partisan Edge on Gay Rights

In the coverage of gay rights, there is a decided partisan edge that filters out facts that might undercut the homosexual rights cause. Although it prides itself on understanding nontraditional cultures, such as that of gay people, American journalism shows far less readiness or ability to extend respect to or curiosity about traditional cultures, like those of the military and the churches.

The script on homosexuals also tends to depict any objections to gay causes—however well-grounded in constitutional, health, moral, or institutional traditions—as outright bigotry to be portrayed cartoonishly. Whether the issue is homosexuals in the military, gay "marriage," or gay clergy, the press has been supportive of the homosexual rights cause.

Jeff Jacoby of the *Boston Globe*, for one, has run afoul of gay newsroom monitors: "I know up front that if I want to write about this topic [homosexual rights], I have to be prepared to run a gauntlet and to jump a lot of hurdles—not among the readers, who I think mostly agree with me, but right here in the newsroom."

One blazing example of partisan reporting involves the refusal of many news organizations to acknowledge that homosexuality plays a role in the sex abuse scandal rocking the Catholic Church [involving priests accused of child sexual abuse]. Ninety percent of the cases of abuse that have come to light involve priests exploiting teenage boys, not girls.

As more stories come to light, it seems that the threat of blackmail kept many church leaders—themselves with skeletons in their closet—from strongly penalizing clerical malefactors, many of them homosexual. Yet the news media are staunch, taking cues from the gay lobby in asserting that homosexuality is not involved and the church's discussion of screening out homosexuals from the priesthood amounts to a witch-hunt.

Affirmative Action

In terms of bias, no issue bears the mark of the new diversity orthodoxy more than the emotionally divisive subject of racial preferences. The ideological bias came through starkly in slanted coverage of the 1996 California Civil Rights Initiative, also known as Proposition 209, which successfully rolled back racial preferences in public-sector hiring and the state's higher education system.

At the very beginning of that initiative, for instance, the *New York Times Magazine* ran a long, admiring articles identifying Patrick Chavis, a black doctor in Los Angeles. The piece cited him as evidence that affirmative action in medical schools was working as it was meant to, by bringing good doctors into minority neighborhoods. Two years later, after Chavis maimed several patients and killed another, the state yanked his medical license for egregious malpractice. The *New York Times*, as well as other news organizations that had put him on a pedestal, never reported it.

The well-intentioned diversity effort has run off the rails for complicated reasons. One is the clumsy bureaucratic programs, such as those favored by the Gannett organization, that have counted stories, sources, quotes, and pictures by race and penalize editors and reporters who don't meet quotas.

Another reason is pandering, as publishers take the business case for diversity too far. Intentionally or not, the editorial side is told which issues to go easy on or warned that certain groups might mount boycotts or protest marches that could hurt the organization.

Still another reason is the multicultural movement's lack of regard for true intellectual and ideological diversity. Newsrooms have long been disproportionately liberal, and the influx of women and minorities tends to reinforce that. As a result, certain unfashionable voices are overlooked or muted, and certain groups feel more empowered in the journalistic shouting match than others.

It can't be emphasized enough, however, that the problem is not an active liberal conspiracy, as some conservatives charge, with left-wingers huddling around the watercooler to decide how to slant that day's news. Rather, it is one of an invisible liberal consensus, which is either hostile to or simply unaware of the other side of things, thereby making the newsroom susceptible to unconscious but deeply rooted bias.

The search for distinct minority points of view and voices has opened the door to ethnic, racial, and gender cheerleading. A disparagement of objectivity as a "white cultural value" has led some journalists of color to have less concern for candor and factuality than for attacking racial stereotypes and a perceived right-wing backlash.

Minority journalists also exert peer pressure on each other. As Michelle Malkin, who dislikes being identified as a "Filipino-American journalist," wrote in a column published just after Unity 99, a conclave of minority-journalist organizations: "Reporters hired because of racial preferences wind up reinforcing each other, leading to groupthink [and] an unspoken mandate of strict political conformity.

"If you don't accept the left-leaning agenda of advocacy," she continued, "you're enabling racism. If you don't support the pursuit of racial hiring goals as a primary journalistic goal, you're selling out."

Finally, racial and ethnic intimidation plays a role in the broader problem. Journalism is a profession that prides itself on its maverick outspokenness and free-spirited regard for skepticism. Yet in today's climate, the subject of bias is practically a taboo, and those who want to raise the issue know better.

As one Washington bureau chief said to me while outlining an orthodoxy on diversity-bred bias in coverage: "I deplore the fact that the issue is so sensitive that reporters don't want to talk by name. I don't want to contribute to that, but I would rather not be noted by name either.". . .

Unintended Consequences

The unintended consequences for our broader civic culture and our growth as a multicultural society should be of concern to us all. Instead of making public discourse more intellectually sophisticated, the journalistic propaganda on diversity has helped dumb it down. Instead of nurturing a sense of public cooperation, through which the public feels the bonds and obligations of shared citizenship, the emphasis on diversity has discouraged it by celebrating ethnic differences and supporting a race-conscious approach to public life. Instead of enhancing public trust—a critical element in the forging of a public consensus on the thorny issues at hand—the media's diversity effort has discouraged it.

Reporting and analysis distorted by double standards, intellectual dishonesty, and fashionable cant that favors certain groups over others actually crimp the very debate they purport to enhance. As one perceptive reporter at the *San Francisco Chronicle* reflected: "The ultimate goal is a society with as much racial and ethnic fairness and harmony as possible, but we can't get there unless we in the press are ready to talk about it in full."

"No reasonable person can claim that the repeal of the Fairness Doctrine has led to a wider diversity of views."

Broadcasters Should Be Required to Air a Variety of Opposing Views

Edward Monks

From 1949 to 1987, the Federal Communications Commission, the government agency that regulates the nation's airwaves, had a Fairness Doctrine that required that radio and television stations air a variety of opposing views whenever political issues were discussed. In the viewpoint that follows, Edward Monks describes how the regulation was abolished in the 1980s under President Ronald Reagan. The political content of talk radio shows and other media programs are now dominated by conservatives who support the views of broadcast station owners and advertisers, he claims, a development he considers harmful to the public. Monks is a lawyer from Eugene, Oregon.

As you read, consider the following questions:

1. How is the radio market of Eugene, Oregon, reflective of national trends, according to Monks?
2. What have been some of the political effects of the domination of conservative views on radio, according to the author?
3. Why are liberal views not heard on radio shows, according to Monks?

Edward Monks, "The End of Fairness: Right-wing Commentators Have a Virtual Monopoly When It Comes to Talk Radio Programming," *Register-Guard*, June 30, 2002. Copyright © 2002 by *Register-Guard*. Reproduced by permission of the author.

O nce upon a time, in a country that now seems far away, radio and television broadcasters had an obligation to operate in the public interest. That generally accepted principle was reflected in a rule known as the Fairness Doctrine.

The rule, formally adopted by the Federal Communications Commission in 1949, required all broadcasters to devote a reasonable amount of time to the discussion of controversial matters of public interest. It further required broadcasters to air contrasting points of view regarding those matters. The Fairness Doctrine arose from the idea imbedded in the First Amendment that the wide dissemination of information from diverse and even antagonistic sources is essential to the public welfare and to a healthy democracy.

The FCC is mandated by federal law to grant broadcasting licenses in such a way that the airwaves are used in the "public convenience, interest or necessity." The U.S. Supreme Court in 1969 unanimously upheld the constitutionality of the Fairness Doctrine, expressing the view that the airwaves were a "public trust" and that "fairness" required that the public trust accurately reflect opposing views.

However, by 1987 the Fairness Doctrine was gone—repealed by the FCC, to which President [Ronald] Reagan had appointed the majority of commissioners.

That same year, Congress codified the doctrine in a bill that required the FCC to enforce it. President Reagan vetoed that bill, saying the Fairness Doctrine was "inconsistent with the tradition of independent journalism." Thus, the Fairness Doctrine came to an end both as a concept and a rule.

The Rise of Conservative Talk Radio

Talk radio shows how profoundly the FCC's repeal of the Fairness Doctrine has affected political discourse. In recent years almost all nationally syndicated political talk radio hosts on commercial stations have openly identified themselves as conservative, Republican, or both: Rush Limbaugh, Michael Medved, Michael Reagan, Bob Grant, Ken Hamblin, Pat Buchanan, Oliver North, Robert Dornan, Gordon Liddy, Sean Hannity, Michael Savage, et al. The spectrum of opinion on national political commercial talk radio shows ranges from extreme right wing to very extreme right wing—there is virtually nothing else.

On local stations, an occasional nonsyndicated moderate or liberal may sneak through the cracks, but there are relatively few such exceptions, This domination of the airwaves by a single political perspective clearly would not have been permissible under the Fairness Doctrine.

One Town's Choices

Eugene [Oregon] is fairly representative. There are two local commercial political talk and news radio stations: KUGN, owned by Cumulus Broadcasting, the country's second largest radio broadcasting company, and KPNW, owned by Clear Channel Communications, the largest such company.

KUGN's line-up [as of June 2002] has three highly partisan conservative Republicans—Lars Larson (who is regionally syndicated), Michael Savage and Michael Medved (both of whom are nationally syndicated), covering a nine-hour block each weekday from 1 P.M. until 10 P.M. Each host is unambiguous in his commitment to advancing the interests and policies of the Republican party, and unrelenting in his highly personalized denunciation of Democrats and virtually all Democratic Party policy initiatives. That's 45 hours a week.

For two hours each weekday morning, KUGN has just added nationally syndicated host Bill O'Reilly. Although he occasionally criticizes a Republican for something other than being insufficiently conservative, O'Reilly is clear in his basic conservative viewpoint. His columns are listed on the Townhall.com web site, created by the strongly conservative Heritage Foundation. That's 55 hours of political talk on KUGN each week by conservatives and Republicans. No KUGN air time is programmed for a Democratic or liberal political talk show host.

KPNW carries popular conservative Rush Limbaugh for three hours each weekday, and Michael Reagan, the conservative son of the former president, for two hours, for a total of 25 hours per week.

Thus, between the two stations, there are 80 hours per week, more than 4,000 hours per year, programmed for Republican and conservative hosts of political talk radio, with not so much as a second programmed for a Democratic or liberal perspective.

For anyone old enough to remember 15 years earlier when the Fairness Doctrine applied, it is a breathtakingly remarkable change—made even more remarkable by the fact that the hosts whose views are given this virtual monopoly of political expression spend a great deal of time talking about "the liberal media."

Restoring Discussion of Public Issues

[David Barsamian:] *Do you favor bringing back the now-abolished Fairness Doctrine, as well as requirements for public interest programming?*

[Ben Bagdikian:] I think it's absolutely essential if we are going to save the broadcasting system from being the Corporate USA broadcasting system. Under the Fairness Doctrine [conservative radio show host] Rush Limbaugh would not be censored. I'm not in favor of that but those whom he attacked would get equal time. That was supposed to be basic in communications law. An interesting thing happened when repealing the Fairness Doctrine came up. I think it was in the late 1960s or early 1970s. Newspapers overwhelmingly editorialized against repeal. At that time, newspapers were only light owners of TV and radio. When it came up again in the 1980s, because then we had media conglomerates in real force, almost every newspaper of any size was in a broadcasting conglomerate, owned radio and TV stations. They editorialized in favor of repeal. . . .

The broadcasters said to the FCC, if you will cancel that, they told Congress, we will be able to increase our discussion of public issues on the air. They repealed the Fairness Doctrine. [Consumer advocate] Ralph Nader did a study. Discussion of public issues dropped 31 percent. So they lied and got away with it.

Ben Bagdikian, interviewed by David Barsamian, *Z Magazine*, September 1998.

Political opinions expressed on talk radio are approaching the level of uniformity that would normally be achieved only in a totalitarian society, where government commissars or party propaganda ministers enforce the acceptable view with threats of violence. There is nothing fair, balanced or democratic about it. Yet the almost complete right wing Republican domination of political talk radio in this country has been accomplished without guns or gulags. Let's see how it happened.

How the Fairness Doctrine Was Abolished

As late as 1974, the FCC was still reporting that "we regard strict adherence to the Fairness Doctrine as the single most important requirement of operation in the public interest—the sine qua non for grant for renewal of license." That view had been ratified by the U.S. Supreme Court, which wrote in glowing terms in 1969 of the people's right to a free exchange of opposing views on the public airwaves:

"But the people as a whole retain their interest in free speech by radio and their collective right to have the medium function consistently with the ends and purposes of the First Amendment. It is the right of the viewers and listeners, not the right of the broadcasters, which is paramount," the court said. "Congress need not stand idly by and permit those with licenses to ignore the problems which beset the people or to exclude from the airwaves anything but their own views of fundamental questions."

Through 1980, the FCC, the majority in Congress and the U.S. Supreme Court all supported the Fairness Doctrine. It was the efforts of an interesting collection of conservative Republicans (with some assistance from liberals such Sen. William Proxmire, a Wisconsin Democrat, and well-respected journalists such as Fred Friendly) that came together to quickly kill it.

The position of the FCC dramatically changed when President Reagan appointed Mark Fowler as chairman in 1981. Fowler was a lawyer who had worked on Reagan's campaign, and who specialized in representing broadcasters. Before his nomination, which was well received by the broadcast industry, Fowler had been a critic of the Fairness Doctrine. As FCC chairman, Fowler made clear his opinion that "the perception of broadcasters as community trustees should be replaced by a view of broadcasters as marketplace participants." He quickly put in motion of series of events leading to two court cases that eased the way for repeal of the Fairness Doctrine six years later.

At almost the same time, Sen. Bob Packwood, R-Ore.,

who became chairman of the Commerce Committee when Republicans took control of the Senate in 1981, began holding hearings designed to produce "evidence" that the Fairness Doctrine did not function as intended.

Packwood also established the Freedom of Expression Foundation, described by its president, Craig Smith, long associated with Republican causes, as a "foundation which would coordinate the repeal effort using non-public funds, and which could provide lobbyists, editorialists and other opinion leaders with needed arguments and evidence."

Major contributors to the foundation included the major broadcast networks, as well as Philip Morris, Anheuser-Busch, AT&T and TimesMirror.

Packwood and the foundation argued that the Fairness Doctrine chilled or limited speech because broadcasters became reluctant to carry opinion-oriented broadcasts out of fear that many organizations or individuals would demand the opportunity to respond. The argument, which appealed to some liberals such as Proxmire, thus held that the doctrine, in practice, decreased the diversity of opinion expressed on public airwaves.

In 1985, the FCC formally adopted the views advanced by Packwood and the foundation, issuing what was termed a "Fairness Report," which contained a "finding" that the Fairness Doctrine in actuality "inhibited" broadcasters and that it "disserves the interest of the public in obtaining access to diverse viewpoints." Congress, and much of the rest of the country, remained unconvinced.

Shortly thereafter, in a 2-1 decision in 1986, the U.S. Court of Appeals for the District of Columbia upheld a new FCC rule refusing to apply the Fairness Doctrine to teletext (the language appearing at the bottom of a television screen). The two-judge majority decided that Congress had not made the Fairness Doctrine a binding statutory obligation despite statutory language supporting that inference. The two judges were well-known conservatives Antonin Scalia and Robert Bork, each thereafter nominated to the U.S. Supreme Court by President Reagan. Their ruling became the beginning of the end for the Fairness Doctrine.

The next year, 1987, in the case *Meredith Corp. vs. FCC,*

the FCC set itself up to lose in such a way as to make repeal of the Fairness Doctrine as easy as possible. The opinion of the District of Columbia Court of Appeals took note of the commission's intention to undercut the Fairness Doctrine:

"Here, however, the Commission itself has already largely undermined the legitimacy of its own rule. The FCC has issued a formal report that eviscerates the rationale for its regulations. The agency has deliberately cast grave legal doubt on the fairness doctrine. . . ."

The court was essentially compelled to send the case back to the FCC for further proceedings, and the commission used that opportunity to repeal the Fairness Doctrine. Although there have been several congressional attempts to revive the doctrine, Reagan's veto and the stated opposition of his successor, George Bush, were successful in preventing that.

It is difficult to underestimate the consequences of repeal of the Fairness Doctrine on the American political system. In 1994, when Republicans gained majorities in both chambers of Congress, Newt Gingrich, soon to become speaker of the House, described the voting as "the first talk radio election."

Although it is not susceptible to direct proof, it seems clear to me that if in communities throughout the United States [Democratic candidate] Al Gore had been the beneficiary of thousands of hours of supportive talk show commentary and [Republican] George W. Bush the victim of thousands of hours of relentless personal and policy attack, the vote would have been such that not even the U.S. Supreme Court could have made Bush president.[1]

Broadcasters Favor Conservative Views

Broadcasters' choice to present conservative views is not purely about attracting the largest number of listeners. Broadcasters and their national advertisers tend to be wealthy corporations and entities, operated and owned by wealthy individuals. Virtually all national talk show hosts advocate a reduction or elimination of taxes affecting the wealthy. They vigorously argue for a reduction in income taxes, abolition of

1. In the 2000 presidential election, Al Gore won more popular votes than Bush, but Bush won a narrow electoral college victory in part due to a favorable Supreme Court ruling over disputed election returns in Florida.

the estate tax and reduction or elimination of the capital gains tax—positions directly consistent with the financial interests of broadcasters and advertisers.

Imagine a popular liberal host who argued for a more steeply graduated income tax, an increase in the tax rate for the largest estates and an increase in the capital gains tax rate.

Broadcasters and advertisers have no interest in such a host, no matter how large the audience, because of the host's ability to influence the political climate in a way that broadcasters and advertisers ultimately find to be economically unfavorable.

Hence we wind up with a distortion of a true market system in which only conservatives compete for audience share. Whether the theory is that listeners listen to hear views they agree with, or views they disagree with, in a purely market driven arena, broadcasters would currently be scrambling to find liberal or progressive talk show hosts. They are not.

The beneficiaries of the talk show monopoly are not content. Immediately after he became House speaker, Newt Gingrich led the Republican battle to eliminate federal funding for the Corporation for Public Broadcasting, which, free of some commercial considerations, had broadcast a wider spectrum of opinion. Although not fully successful, that campaign led to a decrease in federal funding for the CPB, a greater reliance on corporate "sponsors" and a drift toward programming acceptable to conservatives.

No reasonable person can claim that the repeal of the Fairness Doctrine has led to a wider diversity of view—to a "warming" of speech, as the FCC, the Freedom of Expression Foundation and others had predicted.

Perhaps it should not be a surprise that the acts of President Reagan, Reagan's FCC appointments, Sen. Packwood, Justice Scalia and failed Supreme Court nominee Bork and the first President Bush should combine to ultimately produce, in my town, a 4,000 hour to zero yearly advantage for Republican propaganda over the Democratic opposition. Nor should we overlook the Orwellian irony that the efforts of an organization calling itself the Freedom of Expression Foundation helped result in so limited a range of public expression of views.

Perhaps the current president [George W. Bush], aware that the repeal of the Fairness Doctrine had the opposite effect of what was publicly predicted by his predecessors and aware that a monopoly on public expression is inconsistent with a democratic tradition, will direct his administration to reinstate the Fairness Doctrine. What about that cold day in hell?

"[The Fairness Doctrine] mandated against controversy and free debate."

Broadcasters Should Not Be Required to Air a Variety of Opposing Views

Part I: Katherine Mangu-Ward; Part II: Joseph Farah

From 1949 to 1987, the Federal Communications Commission's Fairness Doctrine required radio and television stations to present opposing views on political issues. Some members of Congress want to restore the Fairness Doctrine. The following two-part viewpoint presents arguments against such regulation. In Part I Katherine Mangu-Ward writes that the Fairness Doctrine has become outdated in an era where a wide variety of political views can be found on digital and cable television and on the Internet. Mangu-Ward writes for the *Weekly Standard*, a conservative opinion journal. In Part II, Joseph Farah argues that Congressional efforts to bring back the Fairness Doctrine violate the First Amendment's protections of free speech. Farah is the founder of WorldNetDaily.com, an independent Internet news service.

As you read, consider the following questions:

1. How have recent actions by the Federal Communications Commission brought about efforts to restore the Fairness Doctrine, according to Mangu-Ward?
2. Why would restoring the Fairness Doctrine violate the First Amendment, according to Farah?

I

Changes in Federal Communications Commission regulations don't normally capture national attention. But a decision last June [2003] has people who worry about the growing influence of Big Media in a tizzy. [Former president] Bill Clinton frets that "monolithic control over local media will reduce the diversity of information, opinion, and entertainment people get.". . .

It all culminated in a Senate vote on September 16 [2003] to repeal part of the decision by the FCC to relax media ownership rules. The old rules prohibit a company from owning television stations that reach more than 35 percent of homes nationwide; the new rules allow up to 45 percent.[1]. . .

Re-Regulating the Media

But the Senate vote is only the beginning of a much larger campaign for some who have been itching to re-regulate television and radio for the last two decades. By tweaking media consolidation rules, the FCC reopened a debate that started at the commission's creation in 1934. The "fairness doctrine," a set of rules requiring that radio and television broadcast stations present a variety of opposing views, was in effect from 1945 until 1987 (when [Ronald] Reagan's FCC repealed it), and the scuffle over the FCC's latest decision has reinvigorated efforts to bring it back.

Three days after the FCC announced the new rules back in June, Maurice Hinchey, Democratic congressman from New York, released a statement headlined "Hinchey Vows to Reclaim Airwaves for Public." Repealing the FCC's action is not enough, he says. In the coming weeks, he plans to introduce a bill that would reinstate the fairness doctrine not as a mere FCC rule, but as legislation. Though the fairness doctrine is often referred to as the "equal time rule," Hinchey says his bill would not explicitly require equal time, only "more diverse" views on all stations.

The concept behind the fairness doctrine seems innocuous. But in practice, Hinchey's bill would get the FCC into the

1. Implementation of the FCC's proposed rules changes was halted by a federal court in September 2003 pending judicial review.

business of dictating content, and owners of radio and television stations would be forced to broadcast opinions they don't espouse. Aside from a host of First Amendment concerns, critics of the doctrine say it could actually result in more uniformity, not more diversity. If every station offers the same pair of "opposing viewpoints" in order to fulfill its obligations to the FCC, stations will become indistinguishable.

The Broadcast Spectrum

The FCC, which licenses broadcasters to use discrete portions of the broadcast spectrum, has a responsibility to promote the "widest possible dissemination of information from diverse and antagonistic sources," according to its charter. The broadcast spectrum is a limited public resource, say defenders of the fairness doctrine, and to ensure that it meets the demands of its charter, the FCC must react to this scarcity by monitoring content.

But it turns out we have a lot more spectrum than we thought, and a lot less demand for it than anticipated in 1934, during the fledgling days of television. The fairness doctrine was crafted before cable television, digital television, and the Internet relieved demand for spectrum space. The existing rules predicated on scarcity are simply outdated, rendered irrelevant by unforeseen technological advances, according to [FCC chairman Michael] Powell's FCC.

In 1980, there were 75 all-talk radio stations in the country. Now there are more than 1,300. Hinchey dismisses the proliferation of media outlets, saying the "alleged existence of a great diversity" is undermined by the fact that the outlets "are increasingly controlled by a limited number of organizations and people."

Crush Rush?

Those 1,300 talk stations, nearly all born since the repeal of the fairness doctrine and nearly all right-leaning—with the exception of Pacifica Radio—will be in the thick of the battle over Hinchey's bill. The legislation—which has been called the "Crush Rush" bill (most notably by the king of conservative talk himself, Rush Limbaugh)—would hurt conservative radio the most. But it would also have a chilling effect on political coverage on stations with other formats, says Braden Cox, technology counsel at the Competitive Enterprise Institute, making broadcasters reluctant to address controversial issues for fear of running afoul of the FCC. After all, radio and television stations depend on the FCC for their existence, and can't afford to antagonize the entity that renews their licenses.

Limbaugh, Sean Hannity, and dozens of less popular shows have already begun efforts to stop the reinstatement of the fairness doctrine. And though Limbaugh himself has a large enough audience to guarantee that he won't be kicked off the air, his second- and third-tier colleagues are less secure, and he's more than willing to put up a fight to keep them from getting cancelled to make room for mandatory "opposing view" programming.

Congressmen who support Hinchey's bill may be "sorry they pulled this tiger's tail," says James Gattuso, research fellow in regulatory policy at the Heritage Foundation, when the talk radio hosts "really get geared up." They will be fighting for their livelihood, and there won't be any law (yet) that says they have to give airtime to the other side of the argument.

II

"Congress shall make no law respecting an establishment of religion, or prohibiting the free exercise thereof; or abridging the freedom of speech, or of the press; or the right of the people peaceably to assemble, and to petition the government for a redress of grievances."
—*First Amendment to the U.S. Constitution*

I guess it's time for another lesson on the First Amendment.

For the life of me, I can't figure out what's so difficult to understand about these 45 words—most of them only one syllable.

Yet, lately, they have been misconstrued, misunderstood, misapplied, ignored, distorted and turned upside down and around more than would seem possible—without being purposeful.

Freedom of Speech

Today's lesson is on "freedom of speech."

Let's be clear that the First Amendment didn't invent the

notion of freedom of speech. Instead, the founders who wrote the Constitution and crafted the Bill of Rights understood our freedoms, our individual rights, our personal liberties were inalienable—meaning they derived not from government decree, but from the Creator of the universe and His natural laws.

Ending the FCC's Power over Content

The Communications Act of 1934 gives the Federal Communications Commission power to regulate broadcast licensees in the "public interest." Over the years, the FCC has employed that broad, undefined power to enact an extraordinary series of content controls.

Early in the 1940s the FCC actually forbade broadcasters to editorialize. Then, from 1949 until 1987, the Fairness Doctrine was imposed on radio and television stations. Broadcasters covering controversial issues of public importance were required to offer their facilities to those with opposing views. So broadcasters stayed away from controversy. The FCC repealed the Fairness Doctrine in 1987. Since then, there has been a stunning increase in the amount of informational programming on radio and television.

Cato Institute, *Cato Handbook for Congress*, 1997.

The Constitution was designed not to create rights or privileges for Americans, but to guarantee that a future government would not trespass on our God-given freedoms.

Freedom of speech is one of those God-given rights. But the Congress of the United States, despite a clear prohibition against abridging that right, is indeed considering just such an illegal, immoral, unconstitutional action.

The Fairness Doctrine

I'm talking about an effort to bring back the so-called "Fairness Doctrine"—abandoned in 1987.

The rule required radio and television stations to provide "balanced" coverage. But, like most efforts by government, it had exactly the opposite effect. Like most efforts by government, it also had very negative unintended consequences.

By requiring "balance," it mandated against controversy and free debate. In 1980, seven years before the "Fairness

Doctrine" was abandoned, there were 75 talk-radio stations in America. Today, there are 1,300.

If the "Fairness Doctrine" is resurrected, that number will shrink, once again, as station owners decide it is simply too much trouble to ensure balance and "equal time" for every imaginable opposing opinion.

And that's precisely why some of the proponents of this legislation are pushing it. They want to see an end to the era of [radio talk show host] Rush Limbaugh. They want to silence the likes of [radio host] Michael Savage. They would like to see the day when radio stations across America are afraid to take Joseph Farah's new radio show.

It might seem like this is a no-brainer—given President [George W.] Bush has already suggested he would veto any bill that brings back the old, discredited, abandoned, speech-squelching Federal Communications Commission rules. But, believe it or not, Republicans in the House of Representatives are about 40 votes shy of the 146 needed to sustain the president's threatened veto. Likewise, opponents in the Senate are worried about having enough support simply to sustain a presidential veto. That's how shaky is our foundation of freedom of speech in this country right now.

A vote here or a vote there could end another constitutionally guaranteed, God-given right.

In other words, it's not just Democrats who want to end free speech as we know it in this country, the Republicans are ready to fall on that sword as well.

Could it be a result of misunderstanding? Could it be that our elected leaders have simply failed to read the First Amendment lately? Could it be they don't understand those simple words?

I don't think so. Both parties regularly violate the Constitution without so much as a second thought. No matter what the end result of this debate, it's clear the debate should not even be taking place—because Congress has no power to curtail free speech.

But let the people be aware of what is happening. When illegitimate authority rears its ugly head, it's time to take our country back.

Periodical Bibliography

The following articles have been selected to supplement the diverse views presented in this chapter.

Eric Alterman	"What Liberal Media?" *Nation*, February 24, 2003.
Brian C. Anderson	"We're Not Losing the Culture Wars Anymore," *City Journal*, Autumn 2003.
James Bowman	"'Media Bias' Revisited," *New Criterion*, January 2003.
Jonathan Chait	"How Political Journalists Get the Story Wrong," *New Republic*, November 10, 2003.
Brent Cunningham	"Re-Thinking Objectivity: In a World of Spin, Our Awkward Embrace of an Ideal Can Make Us Passive Recipients of the News," *Columbia Journalism Review*, July/August 2003.
Economist	"Media Madness; Broadcasting Regulation," September 13, 2003.
James Fallows	"The Age of Murdoch," *Atlantic Monthly*, September 2003.
Neal Gabler	"The Media Bias Myth," *Los Angeles Times*, December 22, 2002.
Eytan Gilboa	"Television News and U.S. Foreign Policy," *Harvard International Journal of Press/Politics*, Fall 2003.
Jonah Goldberg	"Big Dumb Lie," *American Enterprise*, July/August 2003.
Reed Irvine	"This Just In: Liberal Media Bias Is Alive and Well," *Insight on the News*, January 28, 2002.
Michael Kinsley	"Media Bias—Once a Sin, Now a Virtue," *Los Angeles Times*, November 9, 2001.
William Powers	"The Poignant Press," *National Journal*, November 21, 2003.
Raymond Schroth	"Rooting Out the Media 'Bias,'" *National Catholic Reporter*, June 21, 2002.
Jacob Sullum	"Rules of the Air," *Reason*, October 17, 2000.
Makani Themba-Nixon and Nan Rubin	"Speaking for Ourselves: A Movement Led by People of Color Seeks Media Justice—Not Just Media Reform," *Nation*, November 17, 2003.
Karl Zinsmeister	"Jayson Blair's World and Iraq," *American Enterprise*, July/August 2003.

CHAPTER 2

Is Concentration of Media Ownership a Serious Problem?

Chapter Preface

The Federal Communications Commission (FCC) is an independent government agency created in 1934 to regulate the nation's public airwaves and communications system. Its commissioners, who are appointed by the U.S. president to serve five-year terms, have the power to grant and revoke licenses to radio and television stations. For decades the FCC has used its control of the public airwaves to impose various rules restricting media ownership. A 1941 rule barred companies from owning more than a handful of television stations. A 1970 FCC rule barred companies from owning radio and TV stations in the same market, while in 1975 the FCC banned cross-ownership of a newspaper and broadcast outlet in the same market. The rationale behind these and other regulations was to encourage competition and prevent single individuals or companies from monopolizing the media and exerting too much control over what the public could read and hear in the mass media.

However, the explosion of cable channels, satellite networks, and the Internet has led some to believe that the FCC rules limiting media ownership are obsolete. Beginning in the 1980s, many of the rules governing media ownership have been relaxed or restricted. In 1985 the FCC increased the number of television stations that one person or entity could own. The 1996 Telecommunications Act lifted many of the ownership restrictions on radio stations, enabling some companies to accumulate hundreds of stations. The 1996 law also required the FCC to revisit ownership rules every two years and repeal or modify regulations no longer in the public interest. On June 2, 2003, a majority of FCC commissioners voted to loosen some regulations, increasing the number of television stations that broadcast networks could own and enabling more companies to own multiple television stations. It also lifted its ban preventing companies from owning both a newspaper and broadcast media outlets in the same market. (Implementation of the FCC's decision was halted by a federal court in September 2003 pending judicial review.)

The FCC's decision was made over the objections of a diverse coalition of Republican and Democrat lawmakers, and groups ranging from the National Rifle Association (NRA) to the National Organization for Women (NOW). Opponents of deregulation argue that the commission's action threatens American democracy and media diversity by placing too much of the media under the control of a few corporations. They also maintain that local communities will lose control of their own media coverage. Former *CBS News* anchorman Walter Cronkite expressed concern that "the gathering of more and more outlets under one owner clearly can be an impediment to a free and independent press."

Despite these concerns, deregulation of the media appears to be an established trend that enjoys the support of President George W. Bush among others. The viewpoints in this chapter provide various perspectives on media ownership and the proper role of the FCC. As the controversies of the FCC's latest rulings indicate, many Americans worry about the possibility that large corporations have too much power in controlling their access to information.

> "In short, the news divisions of the media cartel appear to work against the public interest—and for their parent companies, their advertisers and the Bush Administration."

Media Monopolies Are a Serious Problem

Mark Crispin Miller

Mark Crispin Miller is a media critic and professor of media studies at New York University. His books include *Boxed In: The Culture of TV* and *The Bush Dyslexicon: Observations of a National Disorder*. In the following viewpoint he argues that the growing control of the mass media—including television networks, radio stations, movie studios, and book and newspaper publishers—by a handful of large multinational corporations is a harmful development in American society. The interests of the public (especially poorer and working-class Americans) in political debate and serious journalism are being compromised by corporations more interested in making money than in informing the populace.

As you read, consider the following questions:

1. Does Miller describe the problem of media ownership concentration as an old or new problem?
2. How has the landscape of media ownership changed between 1996 and 2002, according to the author?
3. How does the author define what the "public interest" is with regard to the media?

For all their economic clout and cultural sway, the ten great [media] multinationals . . . AOL Time Warner, Disney, General Electric, News Corporation, Viacom, Vivendi, Sony, Bertelsmann, AT&T and Liberty Media—rule the cosmos only at the moment [January 2002]. The media cartel that keeps us fully entertained and permanently half-informed is always growing here and shriveling there, with certain of its members bulking up while others slowly fall apart or get digested whole. But while the players tend to come and go—always with a few exceptions—the overall Leviathan itself keeps getting bigger, louder, brighter, forever taking up more time and space, in every street, in countless homes, in every other head.

A Long Time Coming

The rise of the cartel has been a long time coming (and it still has some way to go). It represents the grand convergence of the previously disparate US culture industries—many of them vertically monopolized already—into one global superindustry providing most of our imaginary "content." The movie business had been largely dominated by the major studios in Hollywood; TV, like radio before it, by the triune axis of the networks headquartered in New York; magazines, primarily by Henry Luce[1] (with many independent others on the scene); and music, from the 1960s, mostly by the major record labels. Now all those separate fields are one, the whole terrain divided up among the giants—which, in league with Barnes & Noble, Borders and the big distributors, also control the book business. (Even with its leading houses, book publishing was once a cottage industry at both the editorial and retail levels.) For all the democratic promise of the Internet, moreover, much of cyberspace has now been occupied, its erstwhile wildernesses swiftly paved and lighted over by the same colossi. The only industry not yet absorbed into this new world order is the newsprint sector of the Fourth Estate—a business that was heavily shadowed to begin with by the likes of Hearst[2] and other, regional grandees, flush

1. Henry Luce (1898–1967) was the founder of *Time*, *Fortune*, and other leading magazines. 2. The flamboyant and controversial William Randolph Hearst (1863–1951), publisher of the *San Francisco Examiner* and *New York World*, was a leading newspaper and publishing magnate of his time.

with the ill-gotten gains of oil, mining and utilities—and such absorption is, as we shall see, about to happen.

Thus what we have today is not a problem wholly new in kind but rather the disastrous upshot of an evolutionary process whereby that old problem has become considerably larger—and that great quantitative change, with just a few huge players now co-directing all the nation's media, has brought about enormous qualitative changes. For one thing, the cartel's rise has made extremely rare the sort of marvelous exception that has always popped up, unexpectedly, to startle and revivify the culture—the genuine independents among record labels, radio stations, movie theaters, newspapers, book publishers and so on. Those that don't fail nowadays are so remarkable that they inspire not emulation but amazement. Otherwise, the monoculture, endlessly and noisily triumphant, offers, by and large, a lot of nothing, whether packaged as "the news" or "entertainment."

Of all the cartel's dangerous consequences for American society and culture, the worst is its corrosive influence on journalism. Under AOL Time Warner, GE, Viacom et al., the news is, with a few exceptions, yet another version of the entertainment that the cartel also vends nonstop. This is also nothing new—consider the newsreels of yesteryear—but the gigantic scale and thoroughness of the corporate concentration has made a world of difference, and so has made this world a very different place.

Let us start to grasp the situation by comparing this new centerfold with our first outline of the National Entertainment State, published [by the *Nation* magazine] in the spring of 1996. Back then, the national TV news appeared to be a tidy tetrarchy: two network news divisions owned by large appliance makers/weapons manufacturers (CBS by Westinghouse, NBC by General Electric), and the other two bought lately by the nation's top purveyors of Big Fun (ABC by Disney, CNN [Cable News Network] by Time Warner). Cable was still relatively immature, so that, of its many enterprises, only CNN competed with the broadcast networks' short-staffed newsrooms; and its buccaneering founder, Ted Turner, still seemed to call the shots from his new aerie at Time Warner headquarters.

The Telejournalistic Firmament

Today [January 2002] the telejournalistic firmament includes the meteoric Fox News Channel, as well as twenty-six television stations owned outright by Rupert Murdoch's News Corporation (which holds majority ownership in a further seven). Although ultimately thwarted in his bid to buy DirecTV and thereby dominate the US satellite television market, Murdoch wields a pervasive influence on the news—and not just in New York, where he has two TV stations, a major daily (the faltering *New York Post*) *and* the Fox News Channel, whose inexhaustible platoons of shouting heads attracts a fierce plurality of cable-viewers. Meanwhile, Time Warner has now merged with AOL—so as to own the cyberworks through which to market its floodtide of movies, ball games, TV shows, rock videos, cartoons, standup routines and (not least) bits from CNN, CNN Headline News, CNNfn (devised to counter GE's CNBC) and CNN/*Sports Illustrated* (a would-be rival to Disney's ESPN franchise). While busily cloning CNN, the parent company has also taken quiet steps to make it more like Fox. . . .

Whereas five years ago the clueless Westinghouse owned CBS, today the network is a property of the voracious Viacom—matchless cable occupier (UPN, MTV, MTV2, VHl, Nickelodeon, the Movie Channel, TNN, CMT, BET, 50 percent of Comedy Central, etc.), radio colossus (its Infinity Broadcasting—home to Howard Stern *and* Don Imus—owns 184 stations), movie titan (Paramount Pictures), copious publisher (Simon & Schuster, Free Press, Scribner), a big deal on the web and one of the largest US outdoor advertising firms. Under Viacom, CBS News has been obliged to help sell Viacom's product—in 2000, for example, devoting epic stretches of *The Early Show* to what lately happened on *Survivor* (CBS). Of course, such synergistic bilge is commonplace, as is the tendency to dummy up on any topic that the parent company (or any of its advertisers) might want stifled. These journalistic sins have been as frequent under "longtime" owners Disney and GE as under Viacom and Fox. . . .

Such is the telejournalistic landscape at the moment—and soon it will mutate again, if [President George W.] Bush's FCC [Federal Communications Commission] delivers for its giant clients. On September 13, [2001,] when the minds of the American people were on something else, the commission's GOP majority voted to "review" the last few rules preventing perfect oligopoly. They thus prepared the ground for allowing a single outfit to own both a daily paper and a TV station in the same market—an advantage that was outlawed in 1975. (Even then, pre-existing cases of such ownership were grandfathered in, and any would-be owner could get that rule waived.) That furtive FCC "review" also portended the elimination of the cap on the percentage of US households that a single owner might reach through its TV stations. Since the passage of the Telecommunications Act of 1996, the limit had been 35 percent. Although that most indulgent bill was dictated by the media giants themselves, its restrictions are too heavy for this FCC, whose chairman, Michael Powell, has called regulation per se "the oppressor."

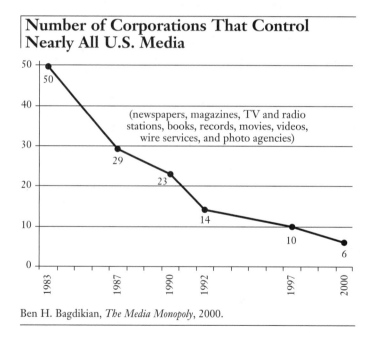

Number of Corporations That Control Nearly All U.S. Media

(newspapers, magazines, TV and radio stations, books, records, movies, videos, wire services, and photo agencies)

Ben H. Bagdikian, *The Media Monopoly*, 2000.

And so, unless there's some effective opposition, the several-headed vendor that now sells us nearly all our movies, TV, radio, magazines, books, music and web services will soon be selling us our daily papers, too—for the major dailies have, collectively, been lobbying energetically for that big waiver, which stands to make their owners even richer (an expectation that has no doubt had a sweetening effect on coverage of the Bush Administration). Thus the largest US newspaper conglomerates—the *New York Times*, the *Washington Post*, Gannett, Knight-Ridder and the Tribune Co.—will soon be formal partners with, say, GE, Murdoch, Disney and/or AT&T; and then the lesser nationwide chains (and the last few independents) will be ingested, too, going the way of most US radio stations. America's cities could turn into informational "company towns," with one behemoth owning all the local print organs—daily paper(s), alternative weekly, city magazine—as well as the TV and radio stations, the multiplexes and the cable system. . . . While such a setup may make economic sense, as anticompetitive arrangements tend to do, it has no place in a democracy, where the people have to know more than their masters want to tell them.

That imperative demands reaffirmation at this risky moment, when much of what the media cartel purveys to us is propaganda, commercial or political, while no one in authority makes mention of "the public interest"—except to laugh it off. "I have no idea," Powell cheerily replied at his first press conference as chairman, when asked for his own definition of that crucial concept. "It's an empty vessel in which people pour in whatever their preconceived views or biases are." Such blithe obtuseness has marked all his public musings on the subject. In a speech before the American Bar Association in April 1998, Powell offered an ironic little riff about how thoroughly he doesn't get it: "The night after I was sworn in [as a commissioner], I waited for a visit from the angel of the public interest. I waited all night, but she did not come." On the other hand, Powell has never sounded glib about his sacred obligation to the corporate interest. Of his decision to move forward with the FCC vote just two days after [the terrorist attacks of September 11, 2001], Powell spoke as if that sneaky move had been a gesture in the spirit of Patrick Henry: "The flame of the American ideal may flicker, but it will never be extinguished. We will do our small part and press on with our business, solemnly, but resolutely."

Certainly the FCC has never been a democratic force,

whichever party has been dominant. [President] Bill Clinton championed the disastrous Telecom Act of 1996 and otherwise did almost nothing to impede the drift toward oligopoly. . . .

What is unique to Michael Powell, however, is the showy superciliousness with which he treats his civic obligation to address the needs of people other than the very rich. That spirit has shone forth many times—as when the chairman genially compared the "digital divide" between the information haves and have-nots to a "Mercedes divide" between the lucky few who can afford great cars and those (like him) who can't. In the intensity of his pro-business bias, Powell recalls Mark Fowler, head of [President Ronald] Reagan's FCC, who famously denied his social obligations by asserting that TV is merely "an appliance," "a toaster with pictures.". . .

The Public Interest

Although such flippancies are hard to take, they're also easy to refute, for there is no rationale for such an attitude. Take "the public interest"—an ideal that really isn't hard to understand. A media system that enlightens us, that tells us everything we need to know pertaining to our lives and liberty and happiness, would be a system dedicated to the public interest. Such a system would not be controlled by a cartel of giant corporations, because those entities are ultimately hostile to the welfare of the people. Whereas we need to know the truth about such corporations, they often have an interest in suppressing it (as do their advertisers). And while it takes much time and money to find out the truth, the parent companies prefer to cut the necessary costs of journalism, much preferring the sort of lurid fare that can drive endless hours of agitated jabbering. . . . The cartel's favored audience, moreover, is that stratum of the population most desirable to advertisers—which has meant the media's complete abandonment of working people and the poor. And while the press must help protect us against those who would abuse the powers of government, the oligopoly is far too cozy with the White House and the Pentagon, whose faults, and crimes, it is unwilling to expose. The media's big bosses want big favors from the state, while the reporters are afraid to risk annoying their best sources. Because of such politeness (and, of course, the current panic in the air), the US coverage of this government is just a bit more edifying than the local newscasts in Riyadh [Saudi Arabia].

Against the daily combination of those corporate tendencies—conflict of interest, endless cutbacks, endless trivial pursuits, class bias, deference to the king and all his men—the public interest doesn't stand a chance. Despite the stubborn fiction of their "liberal" prejudice, the corporate media have helped deliver a stupendous one-two punch to this democracy. . . . Last year [2000], they helped subvert the presidential race, first by prematurely calling it for Bush, regardless of the vote—a move begun by Fox, then seconded by NBC, at the personal insistence of Jack Welch, CEO of General Electric. Since the coup, the corporate media have hidden or misrepresented the true story of the theft of that election.[3]

And having justified [Bush's] coup, the media continue to betray American democracy. Media devoted to the public interest would investigate the poor performance by the CIA, the FBI, the FAA [Federal Aviation Administration] and the CDC [Centers for Disease Control and Prevention] so that those agencies might be improved for our protection—but the news teams (just like Congress) haven't bothered to look into it. So, too, in the public interest, should the media report on *all* the current threats to our security—including those far-rightists targeting abortion clinics and, apparently, conducting bioterrorism; but the telejournalists are unconcerned (just like [Attorney General] John Ashcroft). So should the media highlight, not play down, this government's attack on civil liberties—the mass detentions, secret evidence, increased surveillance, suspension of attorney-client privilege, the encouragements to spy, the warnings not to disagree, the censored images, sequestered public papers, unexpected visits from the Secret Service and so on. And so should the media not parrot what the Pentagon says about

---

3. Al Gore had conceded the 2000 presidential election to George W. Bush on the night of the vote, only to retract it when it became clear that media reports saying Bush had won the state of Florida were premature and that the race was too close to call. After weeks of vote recounts, legal and political maneuvering, and a controversial Supreme Court decision, George W. Bush was declared the winner, even though Gore had received more popular votes nationwide.

the current war, because such prettified accounts make us complacent and preserve us in our fatal ignorance of what people really think of us—and why—beyond our borders. And there's much more— about the stunning exploitation of the tragedy, especially by the Republicans; about the links between the Bush and the [terrorist Osama] bin Laden families; about the ongoing shenanigans in Florida—that the media would let the people know, if they were not (like Michael Powell) indifferent to the public interest.

In short, the news divisions of the media cartel appear to work *against* the public interest—and *for* their parent companies, their advertisers and the Bush Administration. The situation is completely un-American. It is the purpose of the press to help us run the state, and not the other way around. As citizens of a democracy, we have the right and obligation to be well aware of what is happening, both in "the homeland" and the wider world. Without such knowledge we cannot be both secure and free. We therefore must take steps to liberate the media from oligopoly, so as to make the government our own.

"Media monopoly is not a legitimate threat in a free society because citizens are always free to establish new media outlets, and investors are free to fund them."

Fears of Media Monopolies Are Misplaced

Adam Thierer and Clyde Wayne Crews Jr.

Adam Thierer and Clyde Wayne Crews Jr. are research scholars with the Cato Institute, a libertarian policy research institute. They are also the authors of *What's Yours Is Mine: Open Access and the Rise of Infrastructure Socialism* and *Who Rules the Net?* In the viewpoint that follows, they dismiss fears that concentration of media ownership harms American society. They argue that the state of media diversity and competition in the United States has greatly improved in recent decades due to the rise of cable and satellite television and other technological advances, and that Americans remain free to patronize or even establish new media outlets.

As you read, consider the following questions:

1. What do proponents of media ownership rules really want, according to Thierer and Crews?
2. How many television channels could a family tune in to in 1973 compared with today?
3. Why should government restrictions, not media monopolies, be considered the true threat to democracy and free speech, according to Thierer and Crews?

Despite the First Amendment prohibition on restricting private speech, arbitrary caps and quotas have long governed how many newspapers and radio and TV stations a given company can own. On June 2 [2003], the Federal Communications Commission slightly loosened those restrictions, unleashing hysteria from opponents who believe our thoughts are being programmed by a handful of media barons. But such conspiratorial "puppet-master" theories of media manipulation are misplaced. The real media masters in America are the viewers and listeners who demand and receive an ever-broadening array of information and entertainment choices.

Despite claims about the death of diversity, localism, and democracy, what proponents of ownership rules really advocate is their own version of media control and, ultimately, control of content and information. One cannot claim to support democracy and choice and simultaneously support centralized governmental control of the size or nature of private media outlets. Moreover, information is not "monopolizable" in a free society, where government does not practice censorship, and thus there is no such thing as a "media monopoly" unanswerable to the rest of society and the economy potentially arrayed against it. Government's energy is best directed at its own regulatory policies that artificially generate scarcity of bandwidth and spectrum, which can and do stand in the way of new voices.

Information Overload

Misplaced Fears of Media Monopoly. Considering the dismal state of media competition and diversity just 20 to 30 years ago, today's world is characterized by information abundance, not scarcity. Today the media are far less concentrated and more competitive than 30 years ago. Consider two families, living in 1973 versus 2003, and their available media and entertainment options. The 1973 family could flip through three major network television stations or tune in to a PBS station or a UHF channel or two. By comparison, today's families can take advantage of a 500-plus channel universe of cable and satellite-delivered options, order movies on demand, and check out a variety of specialized news, sports, or entertainment programming—in addition to those same three networks.

Today's family also has far more to choose from on the radio. Seven thousand stations existed in 1970 nationwide. Today more than 13,000 stations exist and subscription-based music services are delivered uninterrupted nationwide via digital satellite. And then, of course, there's the Internet and the cornucopia of communications, information, and entertainment services the Web offers. Today, the Internet gives every man, woman, and child the ability to be a one-person publishing house or broadcasting station and to communicate with the entire planet or break news of their own. . . . Today, the library comes to us as the Net places a world of information at our fingertips. And while the 1973 family could read the local newspaper together, today's families can view thousands of newspapers from communities across the planet.

Popularity Is Not Monopoly

Some say the problem is media concentration, and point out that only five companies control 80 percent of what we see and hear. In reality, those five companies own only 25 percent of more than 300 broadcast, satellite and cable channels, but because of their popularity, 80 percent of the viewing audience chooses to watch them. Popularity is not synonymous with monopoly. A competitive media marketplace must be our fundamental goal, but do we really want government to regulate what is popular? . . .

Much of the pressure to restrict ownership, I fear, is motivated not by worries about concentration, but by a desire to affect content. And some proposals to reduce concentration risk having government promote or suppress particular viewpoints.

Michael K. Powell, *New York Times*, July 28, 2003.

Timid Tweaking of the Rules. While America's mass media marketplace is evolving rapidly, the same cannot be said for the rules governing it. Despite the uproar, the FCC's June 2 ruling represented a meager liberalization effort. The national television ownership cap, which limits how much of the national market can be served by broadcast and cable companies, was bumped from 35 up to 45 percent. Likewise, the restrictions on radio and television cross-ownership in a single market, and on ownership of more than one of the top four stations in given market, have been moderately revised. Significantly, rules preventing a company from owning a newspaper and television station in the same market were largely lifted. But other rules remain. For example, the Dual Network rule banning mergers between the big broadcast networks (ABC, CBS, NBC and Fox) was preserved. A limitation on the number of radio stations a company can own in a local market was even tightened. Media companies continue to be forced to play by a restrictive set of ownership rules that are imposed on no other industry.

Protecting the First Amendment

In revising such rules previously, the courts have recognized that the changes in the media marketplace have given citizens a diversity of news, information, and entertainment options that undercuts the rationale behind many of the current regulations. Moreover, the courts have stressed that the First Amendment remains of paramount importance when considering such restrictions of media. Forcibly limiting the size of the soapbox that media owners hope to build to speak to the American people violates the free speech rights we hold sacred. The interesting question now is whether the courts will accept the FCC's incremental changes to the existing rules, and how Congress will respond. Hearings are already being scheduled [in June 2003] and bills introduced that would roll back the FCC's limited liberalization efforts.

But it would be foolish for Congress to do so. Far from living in a world of "information scarcity" that some fear, we now live in a world of information overload. The number of information and entertainment options at our disposal has almost become overwhelming, and many of us struggle to filter and manage all the information we can choose from in an average day. FCC Commissioner Kathleen Abernathy put it well: "Democracy and civic discourse were not dead in America when there were only three to four stations in most markets in the 1960s and 1970s, and they will surely not be dead in this century when there are, at a minimum, four to six independent broadcasters in most markets, plus hundreds of cable channels and unlimited Internet voices."

Given these market realities and a greater appreciation for the First Amendment rights of media companies, the courts may strike down any attempt to reinstate or strengthen the old rules. Congress would be wise to instead focus its energies on revising cumbersome spectrum policies that artificially limit greater innovation and competition to existing media companies.

Consumers Rule

Big Media or Big Government? Media monopoly is not a legitimate threat in a free society because citizens are always free to establish new media outlets, and investors are free to fund them. The scale and scope of private media organizations is not an appropriate target of coercive public policy, because such policy violates free speech. Government restrictions on ownership are themselves censorship and represent the real threat to democracy. Diversity, independence of voice and democracy do not spring from government control of the means of speech, but from a separation between government and media. Information—which at bottom, is what the debate is all about—is fundamentally not capable of being monopolized by private actors. Information is abundant and constantly being created. Only government can censor or prohibit free speech, or the emergence and funding of alternative views. Citizens need not fear media monopoly, rather, in our modern marketplace, it is the media itself that must live in fear of the power of consumer choice and the tyranny of the remote control.

"The case for changing the FCC's ownership rules is clear. . . . They are likely hurting consumers."

Media Ownership Regulations Should Be Lifted

James Gattuso

James Gattuso, who worked for the Federal Communications Commission (FCC) from 1992 to 1997, is a research fellow at the Heritage Foundation, a conservative public policy research organization. In the following viewpoint, originally written shortly before the FCC decided to relax government regulations restricting media ownership, he contends that government restrictions on how many media outlets one individual or corporation can own are outdated. Originally designed to encourage media competition during an era when there were only three major television networks, such restrictions are unnecessary. The FCC should significantly loosen and perhaps even eliminate its rules limiting media ownership, he concludes.

As you read, consider the following questions:
1. What specific rules is the FCC considering for modification, according to Gattuso?
2. How does the author use the 2003 war in Iraq and the Vietnam War to argue against media ownership restrictions?
3. How can joint ownership of television stations and newspapers benefit everyone, in Gattuso's opinion?

On June 2 [2003], the Federal Communications Commission [FCC] will vote on whether to modify or even repeal its restrictions on ownership of broadcast stations.[1] Opponents argue that changes to these rules would reduce diversity in an already concentrated market—warning that big media "monopolies" are already limiting what Americans see and hear.

They are mistaken. Despite many mergers in the media industry in recent years, Americans today actually enjoy more diversity and competition in the media than at any other time in history, thanks to cable TV, Internet, the licensing of new broadcast stations and other factors.

Rather than media monopolies, consumers face a bewildering and unprecedented amount of choice. Instead, the real danger to Americans is that outdated and unnecessary FCC restrictions will limit improvements in media markets and technologies, limiting the benefits that they can provide.

Media Marketplace Driving Review

A variety of regulations are at issue—including rules limiting how many television stations can be owned by networks, how many TV stations a company can own in a particular market, and common ownership of TV and newspapers in the same city.

Most ownership restrictions, imposed on TV and radio license holders by the FCC, are decades old, dating back as far as 1941, though they have been frequently modified. There are six such rules formally being reviewed by the FCC in the current [2003] proceeding. They are:

1. *The Local TV Ownership Rule*, which prohibits TV networks from owning TV stations that reach more than 35 percent of television households. Originally adopted in 1941, the rule was most recently modified in 2000, when the cap was raised from 25 percent.
2. *The Local TV Multiple Ownership Rule*, which limits firms from owning more than one TV station in a market, or two if there are at least eight other stations and

1. On June 2, 2003, the FCC commissioners, in a 3-2 vote, adopted several rule changes relaxing or lifting previous ownership restrictions, including most of the rules listed in this article.

no more than one of the commonly-owned stations is one of the four biggest in the market.

3. *The Radio/TV Cross-Ownership Ban*, which limits the number of radio stations that can be owned by a TV station owner in the same market, using a sliding scale based on the number of broadcast stations in the market.

4. *The Dual Television Network Rule*, which prohibits any of the top four networks—CBS, NBC, ABC or Fox—from acquiring any of the others.

5. *The Newspaper/Broadcast Cross-Ownership Prohibition*, which bars a joint ownership of a TV or radio station and a newspaper in the same market.

6. *The Local Radio Ownership Rule*, which limits the number of radio stations in a market that can be commonly owned, using a sliding scale based on the number of other stations in the market.

The current proceeding marks the first time the FCC has conducted an across-the-board review of its ownership rules (although many have been reviewed separately in recent years). There are many reasons the Commission has taken up this challenge. First, two national and local TV rules have been challenged by U.S. appeals courts, which have ordered the FCC to modify or provide justification for them. More generally, the FCC is required by the Telecommunications Act of 1996 to review all its rules every other year, and eliminate those found not to be necessary.

Changes in the Media Marketplace

But lastly—and most importantly—the top-to-bottom review was required because of the vast changes in the media marketplace in recent years, and in the decades since many of the rules were initially adopted. At no time was this made clearer than during the recent [2003] Iraq war. Americans following that conflict could choose from a half dozen or so news networks—including three 24-hour news channels on cable.

In addition, nearly limitless news was available on the Internet—from which Americans could follow reports from everything from Matt Drudge to Al-Jazeera TV. And they were doing so in large numbers: according to Pew Research, a majority of Americans with Internet access got information about the [2003] Iraq war online. Almost one out of every six said the Internet was their primary source of news.

Compare this to the situation a generation ago—when Vietnam War coverage meant catching one of the half-hour network news reports, supplementing newspaper or magazine coverage. Or the 1991 Gulf War, in which only one network—CNN—provided 24-hour coverage, and the Internet was virtually unknown.

Reasons for Deregulation

Thirty years ago, American families suffered the malaise of three network TV stations and, if they were lucky, PBS (Public Broadcasting Service) and a few UHF (ultra-high frequency) channels. Only about 7,000 radio stations existed.

Today, there's an information overload, not a lack of it. Families can now choose from 500-plus channels of news and entertainment that are delivered via cable or satellites, in addition to movies on demand, VHS and DVD rentals, satellite radio and nearly twice the number of radio stations as before.

Then there's the Internet. Families are no longer tied to one or two local newspapers: They can read virtually any news organization's Web site anywhere in the world. . . .

Given this rich media environment, isn't it a tad premature to proclaim the death of American democracy? If anything, the marketplace seems to be becoming more competitive, not less.

That's why it's reasonable to . . . deregulate the media environment even more. Deregulated industries, as the United States found out after deregulating the airline industry, become far more efficient and offer customers lower prices than before.

This may not happen quickly, but if so-called consumer groups have an honest commitment to American democracy, shouldn't they want to get the government entirely out of the business of deciding who may own a TV station or a newspaper printing press?

Declan McCullagh, CNET News.com, September 9, 2003.

On the local level, similar increases can be seen, with Americans in most cities and towns enjoying remarkably more choice of media outlets than ever before. In Washington, D.C., for instance, channel changers could only surf four TV stations in 1960. Today, there are 15, plus some 150 cable channels. And 300 more on DBS [Direct Broadcast Satellite]. Radio stations in 1960 numbered 20. Today, there are 50 broadcasting, plus 100 more on radio, and thousands available by Internet.

Media Ownership

Critics, however, point out that the existence of many outlets doesn't necessarily mean more owners. NBC, MSNBC, and msnbc.com are clearly not independent from each other. Media firms today tend to own many outlets—putting broadcast, cable, print and even Internet outlets under the same roof. But despite this expansion of media holdings, ownership concentration has not increased. A study released by the Federal Communications Commission last fall [2002] found the number of separately owned media outlets (including broadcast, cable and newspaper outlets) skyrocketed in most cities between 1960 and 2000—growing more than 90 percent in New York, for instance.

Moreover, the ability to own multiple media outlets can provide substantial benefits to consumers. Most directly, it can help make resources available to provide quality programming. It can provide valuable synergies. NBC, for instance, can use overlapping resources and expertise to provide news via broadcasting, cable and Internet media—increasing the quality of each—and increasing its ability to compete with competitors such as CNN and Fox.

Even joint ownership of the same media in the same market (i.e., owning multiple TV or radio stations in the same market) can provide consumer benefits. For instance—though counter-intuitive—common ownership can actually increase content diversity. The reason is simple—while owners with only one station each may all compete for a lowest-common-denominator market, owners with several stations each are able to target niche markets with different programming on each station. This principle is shown in cable TV—with its cornucopia of targeted channels. There is also evidence it has been at work in radio—where the number of radio station formats increased after ownership limits were relaxed in 1996.

Eliminate Rules Entirely

The case for changing the FCC's ownership rules is clear. They were written in a different era, and don't reflect the diversity and competitiveness in today's media marketplace. And, they are likely hurting consumers, by limiting the ability of media outlets to use resources as effectively as possible. The best course would be for the FCC to eliminate the rules entirely (in which case competition would still be covered [by] antitrust regulation, as it is for most other businesses). It is more likely, however, that the commissioners—in the face of populist rhetoric—will ease the rules, but leave them substantially in place. Such reform could be an important step forward, but also a missed opportunity to completely free media markets from these unnecessary regulations.

"[Proposed rule changes] will stifle debate, inhibit new ideas, and shut out smaller businesses trying to compete."

Media Ownership Regulations Should Remain in Place

Ted Turner

Ted Turner is the founder of the Cable News Network (CNN) and other cable networks. His large media properties were acquired by Time Warner (later AOL Time Warner) in 1996, where Turner served as vice chairman until 2003. The following viewpoint was written shortly before the Federal Communications Commission issued a major decision to relax government regulations restricting media ownership. Turner argues that the growing consolidation of media ownership within fewer and larger corporations is bad for the state of mass media in the United States, in part because it would prevent the rise of future entrepreneurs such as himself. Large media corporations will seek profits at the expense of the public interest, will be more risk-averse and less innovative, and may perhaps even abuse their power by slanting their news coverage and cutting off ideas from public debate, he contends.

As you read, consider the following questions:
1. What obstacles do young media entrepreneurs face today, according to Turner?
2. Why is Turner worried about the media industry being too inhospitable to small businesses?
3. What harmful effects does media consolidation have on journalism and news gathering, according to the author?

On Monday [June 2, 2003] the Federal Communications Commission (FCC) is expected to adopt dramatic rule changes that will extend the market dominance of the five media corporations that control most of what Americans read, see and hear. I am a major shareholder in the largest of those five corporations, yet—speaking only for myself, and not for AOL Time Warner—I oppose these rules. They will stifle debate, inhibit new ideas and shut out smaller businesses trying to compete. If these rules had been in place in 1970, it would have been virtually impossible for me to start Turner Broadcasting or, 10 years later, to launch CNN [Cable News Network].

The FCC will vote on several proposals, including raising the cap on how many TV stations can be owned by one corporation and allowing single corporations to own TV stations and newspapers in the same market.[1]

If a young media entrepreneur were trying to get started today under these proposed rules, he or she wouldn't be able to buy a UHF [ultra-high frequency] station, as I did. They're all bought up. But even if someone did manage to buy a TV station, that wouldn't be enough. To compete, you have to have good programming and good distribution. Today both are owned by conglomerates that keep the best for themselves and leave the worst for you—if they sell anything to you at all. It's hard to compete when your suppliers are owned by your competitors. We bought MGM, and we later sold Turner Broadcasting to Time Warner, because we had little choice. The big were getting bigger. The small were disappearing. We had to gain access to programming to survive.

Many other independent media companies were swallowed up for the same reason—because they didn't have everything they needed under their own roof, and their competitors did. The climate after Monday's expected FCC decision will encourage even more consolidation and be even more inhospitable to smaller businesses.

Why should the country care? When you lose small businesses, you lose big ideas. People who own their own busi-

---

1. The FCC did adopt these rule changes on June 2, 2003; immediate implementation of these rule changes was blocked by legal challenges.

nesses are their own bosses. They are independent thinkers. They know they can't compete by imitating the big guys; they have to innovate. So they are less obsessed with earnings than they are with ideas. They're willing to take risks. When, on my initiative, Turner Communications (now Turner Broadcasting) bought its first TV station, which at the time was losing $50,000 a month, my board strongly objected. When TBS bought its second station, which was in even worse shape than the first, our accountant quit in protest.

Branch. © 2003 by *San Antonio Express-News*. Reproduced by permission.

Large media corporations are far more profit-focused and risk-averse. They sometimes confuse short-term profits and long-term value. They kill local programming because it's expensive, and they push national programming because it's cheap—even if it runs counter to local interests and community values. For a corporation to launch a new idea, you have to get the backing of executives who are obsessed with quarterly earnings and afraid of being fired for an idea that fails. They often prefer to sit on the sidelines waiting to buy the businesses or imitate the models of the risk-takers who succeed. (Two large media corporations turned down my invitation to invest in the launch of CNN.)

That's an understandable approach for a corporation—but for a society, it's like overfishing the oceans. When the smaller businesses are gone, where will the new ideas come from? Nor does this trend bode well for new ideas in our democracy—ideas that come only from diverse news and vigorous reporting. Under the new rules, there will be more consolidation and more news sharing. That means laying off reporters or, in other words, downsizing the workforce that helps us see our problems and makes us think about solutions. Even more troubling are the warning signs that large media corporations—with massive market power—could abuse that power by slanting news coverage in ways that serve their political or financial interests. There is always the danger that news organizations can push positive stories to gain friends in government, or unleash negative stories on artists, activists or politicians who cross them, or tell their audiences only the news that confirms entrenched views. But the danger is greater when there are no competitors to air the side of the story the corporation wants to ignore.

Naturally, corporations say they would never suppress speech. That may be true. But it's not their intentions that matter. It's their capabilities. The new FCC rules would give them more power to cut important ideas out of the public debate, and it's precisely that power that the rules should prevent. Some news organizations have tried to marginalize opponents of the war in Iraq,[2] dismissing them as a fringe element. Pope John Paul II also opposed the war in Iraq. How narrow-minded have we made our public discussion if the opinion of the pope is considered outside the bounds of legitimate debate?

Our democracy needs a broader dialogue. As Justice Hugo Black wrote in a 1945 opinion: "The First Amendment rests on the assumption that the widest possible dissemination of information from diverse and antagonistic sources is essential to the welfare of the public." Safeguarding the welfare of the public cannot be the first concern of large publicly traded media companies. Their job is to seek

2. President George W. Bush ordered the invasion and occupation of Iraq in March 2003.

profits. But if the government writes the rules in a certain way, companies will seek profits in a way that serves the public interest.

If, on Monday, the FCC decides to go the other way, that should not be the end of it. Powerful public groups across the political spectrum oppose these new rules and are angry about their lack of input in the process. People who can't make their voices heard in one arena often find ways to make them heard in others. Congress has the power to amend the rule changes. Members from both parties oppose the new rules. This isn't over.

"What seemed to be a Good Thing—the elimination of government control . . . of the airwaves—turned out to be a very bad thing indeed, at least for the average listener."

Media Ownership Deregulation Has Harmed Radio

Bill Park

In 1996 Congress passed the Telecommunications Deregulation Act that, among other things, lifted many federal regulations on the ownership of radio stations. Prior to 1996, the largest number of radio stations owned by a single corporation was thirty-eight; since then, several corporations have acquired hundreds of radio stations nationwide. In the following viewpoint Bill Park argues that while such a trend has been profitable for a few corporations, it has been harmful to radio as a whole. Listeners have fewer choices in what music they hear, communities have lost local control and input, and employees of radio stations have suffered from downsizing and layoffs. Bill Park is a recording engineer and senior editor at Prorec.com, a website for music recording professionals.

As you read, consider the following questions:

1. How does Park characterize the radio industry in the days of his youth?
2. Why has media ownership consolidation made it more difficult for independent radio stations to compete, according to the author?
3. Why have radio stations started sounding all the same, according to Park?

S ince the late 1920s, it has been all about radio. In the 40's the first rock and roll records were played on the radio and a synergy was created that exists to this day. Rock and roll radio rules the airwaves, and impacts the lives of most Americans at one point or another as they follow their daily routine.

The really cool thing about radio was that it seemed to be a place for rebels. Small owners ran stations the way that they wanted to, playing the music that they wanted to, supporting the causes that they believed in, and catering to their own particular if not peculiar audiences. The parallels to rock and roll are inescapable.

When I was a kid, I lived for the music on the radio. It was my escape from the loneliness of being an American kid living in Germany, unable to speak the language very well, and having a hard time being a stranger in a strange land. The mountains and snows of southern Germany were nothing like the sun and sand of Virginia Beach. At night I could almost warm my room with the heat coming from the tubes on my old mono Bakelite AM radio, some cast-off relic donated by one relative or another.

Because of atmospheric conditions I could often pick up stations hundreds of miles away. I sat in my dark bedroom and listened to the "new" music of what would become the British invasion on Radio Luxemberg and, on particularly lucky nights, one of the pirate radio stations. For those who don't know, in the 1960s five pirate radio stations were broadcasting rock music illegally into the British heartland from ships floating off the coast of England outside of the territorial waters. Their efforts broke the BBC monopoly on what music the British public got to hear, and the BBC was forced to acknowledge existence of The Rolling Stones, The Kinks, The Animals, Them (Van Morrison's band) and the other slightly disheveled R&B bands from the northern provinces and other artists who were changing the meaning of the term "long-haired music.". . .

My love affair with the radio continued through college, and on into my adult life. The most interesting thing about the diversity of the medium though, is that my parents listened to the radio, and their parents listened to the radio. All of my friends listened to the radio, though we all didn't always listen to the same stations. There was country music, there was big band music, soft jazz, oldies, soft rock, hard rock, metal, soul, Christian, Latin, classical, 'classic rock', alternative, polka, other ethnic, and just about any other type of music you can imagine, all available at the twist of a dial . . . dozens of stations in every major market covering every interest that you can imagine.

In my travels I have heard stations that started out playing polkas in the morning, but switched to underground rock in the afternoon, and stations that ran basically a "Green Sheet" on the air ("Lila over at Twin Forks is looking for a tiller. She's got three golf clubs, a used ten-speed, and a bushel of apples to trade. Meanwhile, Clem around Sawmill Run is looking for . . ."). The airwaves were a vast, crowded, jumbled cacophony of free choice and strange ideas . . . much like the Internet is today. . . .

Guerrilla Radio

But the face of radio is changing. Let me tell you a little story.

A very long time ago I was at a high-level meeting at Westinghouse. Westinghouse was one of the largest employers in Pittsburgh. A major corporation with plants and facilities all over the world and its corporate headquarters as well as many research, design, and manufacturing plants in this area, Westinghouse had a long history in many aspects of the corporate world, from air brakes and electronics, radios and air conditioners, furnaces, through white goods (refrigerators, washers, dryers, etc.) and nuclear power plants, both for submarines and to generate cheap electrical power.

But Westinghouse had fallen on hard times. Huge investments in facilities and industries had not panned out, and even ten years after [the accident at the nuclear power plant on] Three Mile Island, *nobody* was building *any* nuclear power plants. The government wasn't building subs. The manufacture of white goods and electronics had moved mostly to offshore companies. Massive investments in technologies and personnel were either losing vast amounts of money, or were barely turning a profit.

The only shining star in the Westinghouse corporate cap was the tiny broadcast division, Group W, which was showing double-digit profits. This was not lost on the Westinghouse executives. But the Federal government prevented any serious expansion into this highly profitable area because of FCC [Federal Communications Commission] licensing restrictions.

In the early days of broadcast radio the FCC set up the rules for licensing radio stations. The FCC was leery of the political power that was exercised at that time by the huge newspaper and magazine publishing firms. Wealthy publishers often touted their favorite candidates in their papers. Sometimes they even created their own candidates, inventing qualifications, and by the power of the press, managing to put their own boys in office.

In order to prevent Big Business from being able to stack the deck in elections and influence public opinion the way that it did at the time in newspapers and magazines, the FCC limited the number of radio and TV stations that could be owned by any one owner. Not a bad plan: more owners meant more diversity, more chance of a difference of opinion, and more choices reaching the public. By preventing a small cartel of businessmen from controlling the media, they were basically helping to insure our freedom . . . something that I find that modern government does seldom and poorly, if at all.

But this protection has been eroding since the 1970s as ownership restrictions have become more and more relaxed.

Fast-forward a couple of years. The FCC approves Westinghouse's purchase of CBS. Westinghouse closes its nonbroadcast facilities. Renames itself CBS. Moves its headquarters to the New York offices of the old CBS. So long Westinghouse, with its tradition of a family-oriented business with products that create a warm fuzzy feeling for your home. Hello, CBS Inc., faceless corporate media Golem, swallowing everything in its path and seeking to control the radio and television revenue streams and content in all the major markets of the US.

This is not a new or unique story. What seemed to be a Good Thing—the elimination of government control and restriction of the licensing of the airwaves—turned out to be a very bad thing indeed, at least for the average listener and particularly for those of us in the business of supplying content. As it turns out, huge media conglomerates have been evolving, with many stations under the control of fewer and fewer owners.

So just what does this mean to these media owners groups?

Control and Money

Well, it's all about control and money. This is a Wall Street play, where corporations are contestants in the most powerful popularity contest in the nation, otherwise known as the stock market.

It works using a complex equation of market dynamics, and strategic buyouts. It almost resembles a magic trick. After all, how can a large corporation with its higher expenses run a radio station at a greater profit than the smaller independent owners?

Well, the smaller owners have a lot less clout. Think about it. You own a station or two, and you are trying to get ad agencies to buy radio time from you, but there are 30 stations in your market, the listener base is split among multiple station formats, and 29 other station owners are angling for the same business. You are not in a good position. Often you have to give heavy discounts on your published ad rates. . . . And you are lucky to see any national advertisers. This is important because the nationals expect to pay closer to 'book' than locals, so you make more money per minute by selling ads to nationals than you do by selling to local advertisers.

Now imagine that you are the sales manager for a company owning a couple of dozen radio stations, and you have a major share of the listeners in several markets and control of those markets. You have national advertisers knocking at your door. Your rates go up. Your profits go up. Your stock prices go up.

And the economics seem to bear out the theory. There is massive prosperity and profit in radio these days. More national advertisers are buying top-dollar ads on more stations, stations are able to upgrade facilities and make capital investments in new transmitters and broadcast equipment, and the events, giveaways, and promotions that stations are able to mount are of truly stellar proportions.

In 1999 radio ad revenue was up 11.7% over 1997, continuing a five-year trend of 5+% or more yearly increases.

The value of the transactions of publicly-reporting owners groups for the two year period covering 1996–97 was 27.3 billion, which is seven times more than the period covering 1993 to 1995. Assets rose from 4 billion in 1995 to 15.4 billion in 1997, which is nearly a four-fold increase in two years.

So with all of this prosperity, what am I bitching about? Success is good, right?

Deregulation Has Damaged Radio

The radical deregulation of the radio industry allowed by the Telecommunications Act of 1996 has not benefited the public or musicians. Instead, it has led to less competition, fewer viewpoints, and less diversity in programming. Deregulation has damaged radio as a public resource. . . .

Market consolidation intended by the act does not serve the diverse needs of Americans citizens. Substantial ethnic, regional and economic populations are not provided the service to which they are entitled. The public is not satisfied and possible economic efficiencies of industry consolidation are not being passed on to the public in the form of improved local service.

Future of Music Coalition, *Radio Deregulation: Has It Served Citizens and Musicians?* 2002.

First, from a practical standpoint they are building a house of cards. In order to provide the requisite earnings after expense numbers that impress the stock market, they have to consistently come up with a profit, The profit expectations grow every year. It is just an artificial number that some corporate bigwig decides upon, having little to do with anything other than impressing Wall Street.

How do they do this?

In part, it is through increasing ad sales and ad rates. But they also cut staff, getting rid of the more expensive talent, and bringing in lower paid or no-pay interns. They are cutting the technical staffs. They are piling more and more hours of work on fewer and fewer people. Employee benefits get reduced or eliminated altogether, particularly for new-hires. Good people leave. Less qualified people fill the gaps, for less money and fewer benefits.

Years ago, in the hard manufacturing sector, the owners tried this system in their attempt to flirt with the sirens of Wall Street. They followed all the same strategies . . . downsize the workforce, replace long-term, highly paid experienced workers with cheaper, less-experienced workers, cut corners, consolidate. And they started to build crap instead of viable products.

What most of them found was that they had to go back to the old ways of doing business, which requires that you build a good product, treat your workers well, satisfy your *customers*, and let the market take care of itself. You cannot have a successful business if your product is crap. When your product degrades, the market will leave you. I don't want to say that modern radio is turning to crap, but it is certainly beginning to smell funny.

Hmmmm . . . if you have been paying a little attention, you may have noticed that there seems to be little difference between the stations as you scan the dial. They are all beginning to sound the same. And you may also have noticed that whenever an upstart station comes to town and starts to make some noise with interesting programming or a new twist on things, it is rapidly bought up and absorbed in the milieu of corporate radio. Fewer choices.

What is happening here?

Now, I had mentioned controlling 'a couple of dozen' radio stations. But the stakes are now much higher than that.

Trends in Ownership

Before the 1996 Telecom Act, the largest number of radio stations owned by any single corporation was 38. Currently [2000], media giant Clear Channel/Jacor Communications owns something over 900 US radio stations, 19 US TV stations, and has interests in 240 international stations and over 700,000 outdoor ad spaces like billboards. CBS/Infinity and AMFM can tell similar stories. This triumvirate controls an awesome number of broadcast facilities and . . . *get this* . . . Clear Channel/Jacor Communications is merging AMFM under their control. This will soon (or may already have) put the control of *lot* of media in the hands of just two large corporations.

Last year 35% of ALL radio ad revenue went to the top three owners groups.

In Rochester, the 14 stations owned by Clear Channel/Jacor Communications had 94% of the ad revenue from their market in 1997.

CBS/Infinity controls what 25% of Chicago's radio listeners hear.

If a given media company can control a market, it can dictate rates, say what will and won't get played, and exercise a tremendous amount of power in the marketplace.

In 1997, 5,222 owners controlled 10,246 radio stations. In 1998, 4,241 owners controlled 10,636 radio stations. That's an 8.7% drop in owner numbers versus a 3.8% increase in the number of stations. The latest information that I could find has the total number of US radio stations to be 12,300.

Up-to-date stats on ownership transfers are harder to come by, mostly because there are stations transferring ownership every day. Between 1996 and 1999 a whopping 4,000 radio stations changed hands. Media conglomerates are involved in the majority of these transactions, and it is eroding the diversity of the medium.

In the time period covering 1995 through 1997, Black ownership dropped 26%, and Hispanic ownership dropped 9%. Not an encouraging sign. . . .

More national ads bought in huge blocks and a rising ad rate means that fewer local businesses can afford to advertise on radio.

With the large media conglomerates eating all the national ad money, it becomes harder and harder for the independent station owner to survive in the marketplace.

More stations under the control of fewer people means fewer people deciding what you get to hear. Now, in the least insidious form this means that you may have to hear the same 20 songs over and over all day long, with the same 20 songs being repeated on all of the stations. But already label reps are complaining that they have cities in which a group of stations owned by Owner's Group A has a recording in their rotation, while Owner's Group B won't play the recording at all. Scary stuff. Obviously, what the listener wants to hear has little to do with what gets played.

And if all of this is not scary enough, Clear Channel Communications has received federal approval to buy the giant SFX. The deal is worth 4.4 billion dollars. SFX controls 120 major concert venues all over the country, and recently purchased the Pantage Theater in Toronto as well as the Ford Theaters in both New York and Chicago, and the rights to a large number of popular touring musicals. They also have sports interests. So now they not only control what you hear on the radio, but they control what artists you can see! . . .

I am appalled by the statistics that I discovered while researching this piece. This whole issue is way past any simple concern of music or recording. Another freedom bites the dust, strangled in corporate greed and the mishandling of governmental powers.

I don't know what to do about it. After all, I also believe in the right of a business to grow, expand, and make a profit. And I am a big-time believer in smaller government and fewer government restrictions.

But I have always looked to the concept of 'The Public Airwaves' as a fundamental freedom. I recognize that the airwaves have a profound influence on our lives, and our sense of behavior, and sense of what is right and wrong. Something is seriously screwed up here, folks.

"Far from being a 'cautionary tale' of the dangers of deregulation, radio has a great story to tell."

Media Ownership Deregulation Has Helped Radio

Lowry Mays

Lowry Mays is the chairman and CEO of Clear Channel Communications, a Texas-based media company. After the Telecommunications Act of 1996 lifted national radio ownership caps, Clear Channel aggressively acquired radio stations nationwide to become America's largest radio company. The following viewpoint is taken from testimony Mays provided for Congress in January 2003. Mays argues that the radio industry was in dire financial shape prior to 1996 and that deregulation has left the radio industry healthier than ever before, to the benefit of both radio listeners and station owners. He rejects arguments that the radio industry is too consolidated, asserting that Clear Channel owns less than 10 percent of radio stations nationwide.

As you read, consider the following questions:

1. What evidence does Mays provide to support his assertion that the radio industry is healthy?
2. How did deregulation help the radio industry's economic performance, according to the author?
3. How does Mays respond to charges that ownership consolidation has led to a decreasing commitment to local listeners?

Lowry Mays, testimony before the U.S. Senate Committee on Commerce, Science, and Transportation, January 20, 2003.

F ar from being a "cautionary tale" of the dangers of deregulation, radio has a great story to tell. The industry is
healthier and more robust today than ever before. And that
just wouldn't be true if radio stations across the country
weren't pleasing listeners each and every day. In fact, according to a recent survey, the industry is doing just that. Nearly
3 out of 4 listeners believe radio does a good or very good job
providing the music, news and information they want to hear.
And 60% said they believe radio is getting even better.

Radio has changed in many ways since Richard Nixon and
George McGovern faced off in 1972, and Don McLean's
"American Pie" was number one on the charts. That was
also the year Clear Channel bought its first radio station in
San Antonio, Texas. I knew very little about the business
then, but I did understand the core principle that makes any
radio station a success. You must delight the listener, every
hour of every day.

That's why, in 1975, we made our radio station the first all
news format in San Antonio. Listeners were drawn to the local news, weather, and sports we offered. And when we
broadcast live from local places of business, listeners would
flock to see our on-air talent in person and learn more about
the merchant's goods and services. Everyone benefited, and
it was great radio.

Benefits of Deregulation

Radio is, without a doubt, healthier today as a result of
deregulation, and the public clearly benefits as a result. Recall for a moment the financial health of radio in the early
1990s, before the passage of the Telecommunications Act of
1996. Competition from cable and broadcast television and
hundreds of newly authorized FM stations had forced half of
the nation's radio stations into the red. Many others were
operating close to it.

In 1989 and 1990 alone, AM station profits plummeted 50
percent, and FM station profits dropped by one-third. Investment capital dried up, causing facilities modernization to
grind to a halt, and stations owners who wanted to sell
couldn't find buyers. Radio stations struggled to compete
with televisions and newspapers, and found it increasingly

difficult—if not impossible—to survive periodic downturns in the local economy. Many radio stations resorted to cutting their news budgets or other local programming. Some eliminated local news departments altogether.

All of that began to change with deregulation. With the ability to own more stations, both locally and nationally, radio companies could create economies of scale and benefit from the substantial cost savings that result. An owner of multiple stations in a market could diversify formats and, for the first time since the advent of television, compete successfully in the total market for media advertising dollars.

From 1975 to 1995, for example, radio labored with only about 7 percent of the total advertising pie. Since deregulation, there has been growth in that share, with radio finally moving above 8 percent in 1999 and continuing to increase in 2000. Radio operators can reinvest those savings in their stations, improving technical facilities, increasing the quantity and quality of local programming, and hiring more and better on-air talent.

In Syracuse, New York, for example, Clear Channel saves approximately $200,000 a year by operating its stations as a unit instead of as standalone properties. We have reinvested much of that savings in the stations, upgrading the WSYR transmitter, acquiring a booster for WPHR, and installing state-of-the-art studio equipment. We increased local news programming on WSYR by one hour a day, and produce the area's only local listener call-in show. WWHT now provides local news, but did not before Clear Channel entered the market.

Deregulation has been good for radio in other significant ways. Today, more stations are owned by minority-owned businesses than in 1996 when the Telecommunications Act was passed. Clear Channel is committed to encouraging diverse media ownership, and I am proud to say that we have been able to make significant contributions toward that worthy goal. In connection with our acquisition of AM/FM a few years ago, we sold more than $1.5 billion in radio properties to minority buyers. That represented one-third of all the stations we had to divest to obtain regulatory approval of the transaction. In addition, we have committed $15 million to the Quetzal/Chase Fund, which invests in minority-owned media. . . . We have done all of this not because of any direct benefit to Clear Channel, but because it is the right thing to do.

Deregulation has benefited listeners as well as owners. Study after study, by academics and market analysts, demonstrate that consolidation has led to increases in the diversity of formats available to listeners in local markets, large and small. One recent study by Bear Stearns found that the number of core formats has risen 7 percent since 1996. It's easy to see why this is true. Owners with several stations are better able to diversify their programming to serve the variety of demographics that are present in the market. That is just what we did in Syracuse, which did not have an urban formatted station when we entered the market. By drawing upon our resources, we were able to target this underserved audience and turn WPHR-FM into a successful urban formatted station.

Deregulation: The Bigger Picture

Despite these benefits of deregulation, which are in evidence in local markets of all sizes, some say that deregulation has gone too far. They say the industry is too consolidated. And they contend that Clear Channel, as the nation's largest operator, has too much market power. Let's stop for a moment and put the numbers in perspective. Let's generate some light to accompany the heat.

Radio is by far the least consolidated segment of the media and entertainment industry. The ten largest radio operators account for only 48 percent of the industry's advertising revenues. Compare that to the recording industry, where the top five record companies control 84 percent of all album sales.

It's also interesting to note that in cable television, the ten largest companies account for 89 percent of the revenues. For movie studios it's a whopping 99 percent. And, though the number sounds large, Clear Channel's 1,200 radio stations represent only 9 percent of all the stations in the country. That means that over 90 percent of the nation's radio stations are owned by companies other than Clear Channel.

When these numbers are evaluated objectively, it quickly becomes apparent that radio does not pose a media concentration threat. In fact, the drafters of the 1996 Act made certain of that by limiting any individual company to a maximum of eight stations per market, and only then in markets containing 45 or more radio stations.

Serving Local Listeners

While radio may have changed in many ways over my three decades in the business, the key lessons I learned from that first San Antonio radio station still apply today. Stations must serve the needs and interests of their local communities, listeners and advertisers alike. Radio is inherently a local medium and always will be. That means Clear Channel —along with nearly 4,000 other owners of radio stations in the U.S.—must continually strive to serve our local communities in the best ways we can.

Some have suggested, however, that the commitment to local listeners has been lost as a result of deregulation—lost in a mad dash of consolidation. Let me assure you nothing could be further from the truth. Listeners want to hear a variety of music, news, local affairs and other entertainment programming that appeals to their individual tastes. And in today's multimedia world, those listeners are very discerning. If they don't like what they hear, they will turn the dial, burn a CD, or download an .mp3 recording that is more to their taste. It's that simple, and that risky to our financial health.

That's why Clear Channel will always be in tune with what local listeners want to hear. One tired song, a commercial that lasts too long, or a failure to provide timely news, weather or traffic, and the listener is gone. After all, radio is the only business I know of where you can lose a customer with the push of a button at 60 miles per hour.

We may have grown from that single AM station in San Antonio into the largest radio operator in the country, but we haven't outgrown our commitment to localism and diversity. Contrary to what some would suggest, our radio play lists are not put together at headquarters, hundreds or even thousands of miles away from the communities in which they are played. Far from it. Our play lists are developed by local station managers, program directors, and on-air talent, and are based on extensive audience research, listener feedback, and our employees' knowledge of local tastes and culture.

While we make sure that our radio stations have access to the highest quality news and information sources, we do not dictate the quantity or content of news and information from our San Antonio headquarters. Our local managers decide how to use the tools we give them to meet the needs of their audience. The result is that over 80% of what airs on Clear Channel stations is produced locally.

Explosion of Radio Formats

Let's set the record straight on deregulation that Congress permitted in 1996. The plain fact is that because of deregulation, local radio stations are more competitive with other media. And it is because of deregulation that consumers have a wider array of formats from which to choose.

From hip-hop to gospel, from all-sports to all children's stations, radio format diversity has exploded.

There are 630 Spanish language radio stations today [April 2003]. Six years ago there were fewer than 400. Fifteen years ago in Washington, DC, there was one foreign language radio station. Today, there are 12. In my book, that's diversity.

Quite frankly, the radio business was in terrible financial shape a decade ago. Some 60% of stations were losing money, and scores of stations went dark because the economics of the business could not justify their existence. Given that backdrop, Congress concluded that radio deregulation was warranted. Lawmakers got it right. Radio broadcasters were afforded the opportunity to better serve consumers. And that is exactly what has happened.

Edward O. Fritts, speech before the Media Institute, April 23, 2003.

We simply couldn't operate any other way. The preferences of listeners vary from market to market, and we must respond to those differences if we are to succeed. That is why a song like "Screaming Infidelities" by Dashboard Confessional received hundreds of spins on our Dallas station . . . but just a handful in Indianapolis and here in Washington, D.C. Standardized play lists just don't exist at Clear Channel.

But we don't just serve our communities by playing the

music our listeners want to hear. Clear Channel stations around the country are deeply involved in supporting and promoting a wide variety of local civic and charitable events. Consider just one market—Syracuse, New York—where Clear Channel stations routinely help the community whenever the need arises. For example, . . . the State of New York cited the Blodgett Library, located in one of the poorest neighborhoods in the country, as a safety hazard. Clear Channel raised over $80,000 in a radiothon to help create the "Dream Center," a state-of-the-art library and dynamic learning center at a local elementary school.

Our local news/talk station in Syracuse, WSYR, produced a ten-part series on child abuse and raised money to help create the McMahon/Ryan Child Advocacy Site. The station also raised $35,000 for the Child Abuse Referral and Evaluation program at University Hospital, and published a guide to help prevent child abuse. The National Association of Broadcasters awarded WSYR its "Service to America" award for this series.

These are just two small examples of the countless number of contributions Clear Channel radio stations make every day to the communities we serve in over 300 U.S. markets. From radiothons to 10K races, our stations help raise money for important charities like breast cancer research, child literacy, and AIDS research, to name a few.

Radio and the Concert Business

I've heard some say that Clear Channel has too much power in the music industry. They say that the combination of our radio stations and our involvement in the live entertainment business, through concert promotion and ownership of concert venues, gives us unprecedented clout. They claim we can leverage those businesses to intimidate artists, force out competing concert promoters, and drive up ticket prices.

Well, I don't know if any of these critics have had the privilege of negotiating a concert deal with Cher. Well, we have—and I can assure you she is not intimidated by us one bit. And the same goes for Madonna, Paul McCartney, and the Rolling Stones. The artists themselves wield monopoly power. After all, there is only one Cher.

The truth is that major artists dictate nearly every aspect of their tours—increasingly large performance fees, choice of venues, tiered ticket pricing, percentage of merchandising, even the color of the roses and brand of bottled water in their dressing rooms. If we can't meet their terms, they won't think twice about signing with any one of the local, regional and national concert promoters that compete with us. And when we do sign to promote a tour, we are often not the exclusive promoter. Many artists split promotion of their tour between Clear Channel and other national or local competitors.

Speaking of our radio stations, let me say clearly, and for the record, that Clear Channel does not use the threat of reduced airplay to force musicians to tour with us or retaliate against competing concert promoters by failing to promote their shows on the air. Anyone who would make such allegations simply doesn't understand our business. The fact is live entertainment accounts for less than 7 percent of Clear Channel's revenue. Radio is the bread and butter of our business, and we simply wouldn't risk the ratings of any station by refusing to play or promote a popular artist who isn't touring with us, or by overplaying a less popular artist who is.

To cite just one example, Britney Spears actually received 73 percent more airplay on Clear Channel radio stations in 2002, when she was touring with a competing promoter Concerts West, than she got in 2001 when she was touring with us. Why? Because Britney Spears was one of America's most popular music artists in 2002, and our radio stations hardly could ignore her songs and still meet the needs of our listeners. Remember, if we are not playing what people want to hear, they will quickly vote against us by pressing another button on their radio. It couldn't be easier—or more risky to our financial health.

Even when the artist is lesser known, we can not, and would not, take advantage of any perceived change in the negotiating dynamic. It is not in our interest to do so. It happens that Clear Channel Entertainment depends on small and mid-size venues for a substantial portion of its revenue, and so we have a vested interest in booking the up and coming artists that frequent these smaller stages. In fact, in 2001 Clear Channel hosted over 3,100 acts, of which nearly 70 percent were staged at clubs and other smaller venues. Of all these acts, two-thirds were not affiliated with a major record label, and almost one-quarter were not signed to any label at all. Like our radio stations, Clear Channel Entertainment is absolutely committed to promoting new artists and their music.

Periodical Bibliography

The following articles have been selected to supplement the diverse views presented in this chapter.

Alex Adrianson	"Who Rules the Media?" *Consumers' Research Magazine*, July 2003.
Eric Alterman	"Bad News, Film at 11," *Nation*, March 10, 2003.
Brooke Shelby Biggs	"Different Frequencies: How Small and Scrappy Stations Survive in the Clear Channel Era," *Nation*, August 18, 2003.
L. Brent Bozell and Gene Kimmelman	"Stop Feds from Killing Local News," *New York Daily News*, August 8, 2003.
Broadcasting & Cable	"Rereg, March! Left, Right, Left, Right," June 16, 2003.
Economist	"The Politics of Big Media: Media Regulation in America," September 13, 2003.
Jennifer G. Hickey	"The Death of Diversity?" *Insight on the News*, June 24, 2003.
David D. Kirkpatrick	"New Rules Give Big Media Chance to Get Even Bigger," *New York Times*, June 3, 2003.
Greg Kot	"Tuning Out: Commercial Radio May Be in Its Worse Shape Ever," *Chicago Tribune*, April 17, 2002.
Bill Kovach and Tom Rosenstiel	"All News Media Inc.," *New York Times*, January 7, 2003.
Stephen Labaton	"It's a World of Media Plenty. Why Limit Ownership?" *New York Times*, October 12, 2003.
Jennifer B. Lee	"Musicians Protesting Monopoly in Media," *New York Times*, December 18, 2003.
Ian Masters	"Media Monopolies Have Muzzled Dissent," *Los Angeles Times*, May 1, 2003.
Robert W. McChesney and John Nichols	"Up in Flames: The Public Revolts Against Monopoly Media," *Nation*, November 17, 2003.
John Nichols	"Musicians Confront FCC over Media Ownership," *Progressive Populist*, June 1, 2003.
Floyd Norris	"Making a Mockery of Media Concentration Rules," *New York Times*, November 21, 2003.

Martin Peers	"How Media Giants Are Reassembling the Old Oligopoly," *Wall Street Journal*, September 15, 2003.
Michael K. Powell	"New Rules, Old Rhetoric," *New York Times*, July 28, 2003.
Progressive	"Free the Airwaves!" December 2000.
Robert J. Samuelson	"The Myth of 'Big Media,'" *Newsweek*, August 11, 2003.

CHAPTER 3

How Do the Media Affect Society?

Chapter Preface

Much of the information people receive over the course of their daily lives comes from the mass media. Each day Americans receive visual and textual information from newspapers, television, radio, and other media outlets. Much of what the media produce, such as commercial and political advertisements, are specifically designed to influence our thinking and behavior. The cumulative effect of the media on individual and social behavior has been the subject of much research and debate.

One criticism of the mass media is that they can create unnecessary anxiety by placing too big a spotlight on "bad" news. Local television news programs typically lead off with the latest crime story. Wars and natural disasters often receive blanket coverage by the television news networks. Fearful stories of crime, terrorism, disease, and other problems are often featured on the covers of newspapers and newsmagazines to sell issues. Joe Saltzman, a journalism professor at the University of Southern California, argues that the "hyped up, media overkill" coverage of dramatic and scary events can make it seem that what are isolated and rare incidents have become national trends. Such overkill creates unnecessary fear and "destroys any rational discussion of the issue being explored," he explains.

An example Saltzman cites is the media coverage of shark attacks in the summer of 2001. When a bull shark bit off a boy's arm on a Florida beach in July 2001, it triggered a series of national and international television news and front-page stories about shark attacks that culminated with *Time* magazine putting a fearsome picture of a shark on the cover of its September 4, 2001, issue. Lost in the coverage were the facts that shark attacks on humans are extremely rare occurrences and that there were actually fewer attacks and deaths in 2001 than in previous years. "Every day, thousands of people swim in the ocean and never see a shark," Saltzman writes, but such reality does not meet "our current definition of news."

How does such media coverage affect public attitudes? Marine biologist George Burgess believes that while more people were becoming increasingly aware that sharks were not the monsters depicted in the movie *Jaws* and that they were in fact endangered species, the media's "summer of the shark" changed all that. A 2003 survey by the National Aquarium in Baltimore found that 70 percent of Americans believed sharks to be dangerous, and that 72 percent believed shark populations were adequate or too high—the opposite of what is true, according to Burgess. "The public's fearful fascination with sharks is matched only by the media's google-eyed gullibility," he says.

The "summer of the shark" is one dramatic example of how media coverage can affect society by shaping the public's perception of events. The mass media, many believe, often create news even as they are covering it. The viewpoints in this chapter examine various controversies about how media stories and images affect the perceptions and behaviors of the American public.

> *"Countless studies have shown that a steady diet of television, movie, music, video game, and Internet violence plays a significant role in the disheartening number of violent acts committed by America's youth."*

Media Violence Causes Youth Violence

Senate Committee on the Judiciary

The links between media violence and youth violence have been periodically explored by various U.S. government agencies, including congressional committees. In 1999, in the wake of a series of violent school shootings, the majority staff of the Senate Committee on the Judiciary prepared a report on media violence, excerpts of which form the following viewpoint. According to the committee, numerous research studies have shown that media violence has detrimental effects on the psychological development of children. Violence in television, motion pictures, and other media can cause children to be more violent, desensitized to violence, and fearful of the world.

As you read, consider the following questions:
1. How much violence are children exposed to by watching television, according to the authors?
2. In what ways do the authors contend that media violence can harm even young children?
3. What concerns do the authors express about violent lyrics in popular songs?

Senate Committee on the Judiciary, *Children, Violence, and the Media: A Report for Parents and Policy Makers*, September 14, 1999.

The statistics are chilling. In 1997, law enforcement agencies in the United States arrested an estimated 2.8 million persons under age 18. Of that number, an estimated 2,500 juveniles were arrested for murder and 121,000 for other violent crimes. According to the FBI, juveniles accounted for 19% of all arrests, 14% of all murder arrests, and 17% of all violent crime arrests in 1997.

While the number of arrests of juveniles for violent crimes declined slightly from 1996 to 1997, the number of juvenile violent crime arrests in 1997 was still 49% above the 1988 level.

James Q. Wilson, one of our foremost experts on crime, has observed, "Youngsters are shooting at people at a far higher rate than at any time in recent history." The Centers for Disease Control and Prevention ("CDC") reports that a survey showed that some 5.9% of the American high school students surveyed said that they had carried a gun in the 30 days prior to the survey. Equally troubling, that survey also shows that 18% of high school students carry a knife, razor, firearm, or other weapon on a regular basis, and 9% of them take a weapon to school. While studies show that the amount of youth violence has started to decline, the CDC warns that "the prevalence of youth violence and school violence is still unacceptably high.". . .

Causes of Violence

Fortunately, our nation's growing alarm carries with it a collective will for finding a solution. Americans know that something is wrong, and they are united in their desire to address the problem of youth violence. Americans also realize that a variety of factors underlie this national tragedy, including disintegrating nuclear families, child abuse and neglect, drug and alcohol abuse, a lack of constructive values, a revolving-door juvenile justice system, and pervasive media violence. . . .

Those who would focus solely on the instrumentalities children use to cause harm surely are mistaken. After all, there are unlimited ways that a child bent on violence can harm another person. Thus, limiting the access of troubled children to firearms and other weapons is but one aspect of a comprehensive approach. The remainder of that approach must address this question: Why does a child turn to violence?

A growing body of research concludes that media violence constitutes one significant part of the answer. With respect to television violence alone, a 1993 report by University of Washington epidemiologist Brandon S. Centerwall expresses a startling finding: "[If], hypothetically, television technology had never been developed, there would be 10,000 fewer homicides each year in the United States, 70,000 fewer rapes, and 700,000 fewer injurious assaults. Violent crime would be half what it is." Plainly, any solution to the juvenile violence problem that fails to address media violence is doomed to failure.

A Culture of Media Violence

American media are exceedingly violent. With television, analysis of programming for 20 years (1973 to 1993) found that over the years, the level of violence in prime-time programming remained at about 5 violent acts per hour. An August 1994 report by the Center for Media and Public Affairs reported that in one 18-hour day in 1992, observing 10 channels of all major kinds of programs, 1,846 different scenes of violence were noted, which translated to more than 10 violent scenes per hour, per channel, all day. A follow-up study conducted in 1994, found a 41% increase in violent scenes to 2,605, which translated to almost 15 scenes of violence per hour. Like television, our cinemas are full of movies that glamorize bloodshed and violence, and one need only listen to popular music radio and stroll down the aisle of almost any computer store to see that our music and video games are similarly afflicted.

Not only are our media exceedingly violent; they are also ubiquitous. The percentage of households with more than one television set has reached an all-time high of 87%, and roughly ½ of American children have a television set in their room. Forty-six percent of all homes with children have access to at least one television set, a VCR, home video game equipment and a personal computer, and 88.7% of such homes have either home video game equipment, a personal computer, or both.

What does that mean for our children? Most children now have unprecedented technological avenues for accessing the "entertainment" our media industries provide. The average 7th grader watches about 4 hours of television per day, and 60% of those shows contain some violence. The average 7th grader plays electronic games at least 4 hours per week, and 50% of those games are violent. According to the American Psychiatric Association, by age 18 an American child will have seen 16,000 simulated murders and 200,000 acts of violence.

Gamble. © 2002 by Ed Gamble. Reproduced by permission.

The Littleton, Colorado, school massacre[1] has spawned a national debate over how to respond to this culture of media violence. In May 1999, a *USA Today*/CNN/Gallup poll found that 73% of Americans believe that TV and movies are partly to blame for juvenile crime. A *Time*/CNN poll found that 75% of teens 13 to 17 years of age believe the Internet is partly responsible for crimes like the Littleton

1. On April 20, 1999, two eighteen-year-old boys set bombs and opened fire on students and teachers at Columbine High School in Littleton, Colorado, killing thirteen and wounding twenty-three before taking their own lives.

shootings, 66% blame violence in movies, television, and music, and 56% blame video game violence.

In response, many, including the President, have called for studies to determine what effect that culture has on our children. Yet, we should not use such studies to dodge our responsibility to the American people. At least with respect to television and movies, existing research already demonstrates a solid link between media violence and the violent actions of our youth. Dr. Leonard D. Eron, a senior research scientist and professor of psychology at the University of Michigan, has estimated that television alone is responsible for 10% of youth violence. "The debate is over," begins a position paper on media violence by the American Psychiatric Association, "[f]or the last three decades, the one predominant finding in research on the mass media is that exposure to media portrayals of violence increases aggressive behavior in children." In the words of Jeffrey McIntyre, legislative and federal affairs officer for the American Psychological Association, "To argue against it is like arguing against gravity."

Studies of Television and Film Violence

It has been estimated that more than 1,000 studies on the effects of television and film violence have been done during the past 40 years. In the last decade the American Medical Association, the American Academy of Pediatrics, the American Academy of Child and Adolescent Psychiatry, and the National Institute of Mental Health have separately reviewed many of these studies. Each of these reviews has reached the same conclusion: television violence leads to real-world violence. The National Institute of Mental Health reported that "television violence is as strongly correlated with aggressive behavior as any variable that has been measured." A comprehensive study conducted by the Surgeon General's Office in 1972, and updated in 1982, found television violence a contributing factor to increases in violent crime and antisocial behavior; a 1984 United States Attorney General's Task Force study on family violence revealed that viewing television violence contributed to acting-out violence in the home; and recently, the National Television Violence Study, a 3-year project that examined the depiction of violent behavior across more than 8,200 programs, concluded that televised violence teaches aggressive attitudes and behaviors, desensitization to violence, and increased fear of becoming victimized by violence. The majority of the existing social and behavioral science studies, taken together, agree on the following basic points: (1) constant viewing of televised violence has negative effects on human character and attitudes; (2) television violence encourages violent forms of behavior and influences moral and social values about violence in daily life; (3) children who watch significant amounts of television violence have a greater likelihood of exhibiting later aggressive behavior; (4) television violence affects viewers of all ages, intellect, socioeconomic levels, and both genders; and (5) viewers who watch significant amounts of television violence perceive a meaner world and overestimate the possibility of being a victim of violence.

Harming Children

The research has also shown that television violence can harm even young children. Researchers have performed longitudinal studies of the impact of television violence on young children as they mature into adults. One such study, begun in 1960, examined 600 people at age 8, age 18, and age 30. The researchers concluded that boys at age 8 who had been watching more television violence than other boys grew up to be more aggressive than other boys, and they also grew up to be more aggressive and violent than one would have expected them to be on the basis of how aggressive they were as 8-year-olds. A second similar study, which included girls, arrived at a similar conclusion: children who watched more violence behaved more aggressively the next year than those who watched less violence on television, and more aggressively than anticipated based on their behavior the previous year. Professor L. Rowell Huesmann, one of the researchers behind these studies, summarized his findings before a Senate committee earlier this year [1999]:

> Not every child who watches a lot of violence or plays a lot of violent games will grow up to be violent. Other forces must converge, as they did recently in Colorado. But just as

every cigarette increases the chance that someday you will get lung cancer, every exposure to violence increases the chances that some day a child will behave more violently than they otherwise would.

Some experts also believe that children can become addicted to violence. "Violence is like the nicotine in cigarettes," states Lieutenant Colonel Dave Grossman, a former Green Beret and West Point psychology professor who now heads the Killology Research Group. "The reason why the media has to pump ever more violence into us is because we've built up a tolerance. In order to get the same high, we need ever-higher levels. . . . The television industry has gained its market share through an addictive and toxic ingredient."

Not surprisingly, many have come to view television and film violence as a national public health problem. The American Academy of Pediatrics, for instance, recently published a report advocating a national media education program to mitigate the negative impact of the harmful media messages seen and heard by children and adolescents. Robert Lichter, president of the Center for Media and Public Affairs, a nonprofit research group in Washington, D.C., has framed the issue in language we can all understand: "If you're worried about what your kid eats, you should worry about what your kid's watching."

Less research has been done on the effect of music, video games, and the Internet on children. Nonetheless, on the basis of both that research and the research findings concerning television and film, experts confidently predict that violent music, video games, and Internet material also will be found to have harmful effects on children.

Violent Music and Lyrics

Few would doubt the overall effect music has on people. In Plato's *Republic*, Socrates said that "musical training is a more potent instrument than any other, because rhythm and harmony find their way into the inward places of the soul, on which they mightily fasten." Music affects our moods, our attitudes, our emotions, and our behavior; we wake to it, dance to it, and sometimes cry to it. From infancy it is an integral part of our lives.

As virtually any parent with a teenager can attest, music holds an even more special place in the hearts and minds of our young people. Academic studies confirm this wisdom. One survey of 2,760 14-to-16-year-olds in 10 different cities found that they listened to music an average of 40 hours per week. Research has also shown that the average teenager listens to 10,500 hours of rock music during the years between the 7th and 12th grades.

Inadequate attention has been paid to the effect on children of violent music lyrics. Although no studies have documented a cause-and-effect relationship between violent lyrics and aggressive behavior, studies do indicate that a preference for heavy metal music may be a significant marker for alienation, substance abuse, psychiatric disorders, suicide risk, sex-role stereotyping, or risk-taking behaviors during adolescence. In addition, a Swedish study has found that adolescents who developed an early interest in rock music were more likely to be influenced by their peers and less influenced by their parents than older adolescents.

With good reason, then, parents are concerned about the music lyrics their children hear. And parents should be concerned. Despite historic, bipartisan remedial legislation by the state and federal governments, it is stunning even to the casual listener how much modern music glorifies acts of violence. Studies show that modern music lyrics have become increasingly explicit, particularly concerning sex, drugs, and, most troubling, violence against women. For example, the rock band Nine Inch Nails released a song titled "Big Man with a Gun," which triumphantly describes a sexual assault at gun point. Such hatred and violence against women are widespread and unmistakable in mainstream hip-hop and alternative music. Consider the singer "Marilyn Manson," whose less vulgar lyrics include: "Who says date rape isn't kind?"; "Let's just kill everyone and let your god sort them out"; and "The housewife I will beat, the pro-life I will kill." Other Manson lyrics cannot be repeated here. Or consider Eminem, the hip-hop artist featured frequently on MTV, who recently wrote "Bonnie and Clyde," a song in which he described killing his child's mother and dumping her body in the ocean. . . .

We must not ignore the fact that these violent, misogynist

images may ultimately affect the behavior and attitudes of many young men toward women. Writing about such lyrics in 1996, William J. Bennett, Senator Joseph Lieberman, and C. DeLores Tucker posed the following question: "What would you do if you discovered that someone was encouraging your sons to kill people indiscriminately, to find fun in beating and raping girls, and to use the word 'motherf——er' at least once in every sentence?" While the authors directed that question specifically to parents, it is best addressed to all Americans.

Examining Video Games and the Internet

Interactive video games and the Internet have become the entertainment of choice for America's adolescents. Nearly seven in ten homes with children now [1999] have a personal computer (68.2%), and 41% of homes with children have access to the Internet. Annual video game revenues in the United States exceed $10 billion, nearly double the amount of money Americans spend going to the movies. On average, American children who have home video game machines play with them about 90 minutes a day.

The video games of choice for our youth are those that contain depictions of violence. A 1993 study, for instance, asked 357 seventh- and eighth-graders to select their preferences among five categories of video games. Thirty-two percent of the children selected the category "fantasy violence," and 17% selected "human violence." Only 2% of the children chose "educational games."

Parents are concerned that the fantasy violence in video games could lead their children to real-world violence. That concern intensified when Americans learned that the two juveniles responsible for the Littleton massacre had obsessively played the ultra-violent video game "Doom." Americans also recalled that the 14-year-old boy who shot eight classmates in Paducah, Kentucky, in 1997, had been an avid player of video games. As the *New York Times* observed, "the search for the cause in the Littleton shootings continues, and much of it has come to focus on violent video games."

Here, too, the concern of parents is justified. Studies indicate that violent video games have an effect on children similar to that of violent television and film. That is, prolonged exposure of children to violent video games increases the likelihood of aggression. Some authorities go even further, concluding that the violent actions performed in playing video games are even more conducive to aggressive behavior. According to this view, the more often children practice fantasy acts of violence, the more likely they are to carry out real-world violent acts. As Professor Brian Stonehill, creator of the media studies program at Pomona College in Claremont, California, states: "The technology is going from passive to active. The violence is no longer vicarious with interactive media. It's much more pernicious and worrisome." Another researcher characterizes such games as sophisticated simulators, similar to those used in military training.

Equally troubling, video games often present violence in a glamorized light. Typical games cast players in the role of a shooter, with points scored for each "kill." Furthermore, advertising for such games often touts the violent conduct as a selling point—the more graphic and extreme, the better. For example, the advertisement for the game "Destrega" reads: "Let the slaughter begin"; and for the game "Subspace," "Meet people from all over the world, then kill them." As the popularity and graphic nature of such games increase, so does the harm to our youth. As Lt. Col. Dave Grossman bluntly warns, "We're not just teaching kids to kill. We're teaching them to like it.". . .

No More Debate

The effect of media violence on our children is no longer open to debate. Countless studies have shown that a steady diet of television, movie, music, video game, and Internet violence plays a significant role in the disheartening number of violent acts committed by America's youth. We must now devote ourselves to reducing the amount and degree of violence in our media and to shielding our children from such harmful depictions.

"There's no evidence that mock violence in media makes people violent, and there's some evidence that it makes people more peaceful."

Media Violence Does Not Cause Youth Violence

Richard Rhodes

Richard Rhodes is a prolific and award-winning author of both fiction and nonfiction works; his books include *The Making of the Atomic Bomb* and *Why They Kill: The Discoveries of a Maverick Criminologist*. In the following viewpoint he challenges the claim that watching violence in the media makes children violent. Studies and experiments have failed to establish a causal connection between media violence and actual violence, he argues. Rhodes also points to some research indicating that media violence may actually have beneficial effects by enabling viewers to discharge pent-up aggression, thus actually reducing violent behavior.

As you read, consider the following questions:
1. Why is it easy to believe that media violence influences behavior, according to Rhodes?
2. How have studies debunking the connection between media violence and violence been received and publicized, according to the author?
3. What are three kinds of messages that media send, according to Gerhardt Wiebe?

L t. Col. Dave Grossman, pale, lean and a little goofy in a bad suit, struts the stage of a high school auditorium somewhere in Arkansas, his home state. He's a man on a mission, a smalltown Jimmy Swaggart, swooping and pausing and chopping the air. He's already scared the fresh-faced kids in the audience half to death, and the more scared they look, the wider he grins. "Before children learn to read," he lobs in one of his rhetorical flash grenades, "they can't tell the difference between fantasy and reality. That means everything they see is real for them. When a three year old, a four year old, a five year old sees someone on TV being shot, raped, stabbed, murdered, for them it's real. *It's real!* You might just as well have your little three year old bring a friend into the house, befriend that friend, and then *gut 'em and murder 'em right before their eyes"*—some of the kids in the audience wince—"as have them watch the same thing on TV, watch someone being brutally murdered on television. For them it's all real. Television is traumatizing and brutalizing our children at this horrendously young age."

A retired U.S. Army lieutenant colonel with an M.Ed. in counseling, . . . Grossman left the Army to dedicate himself to saving America from what he calls the "toxic waste" of "media violence" that is "being pumped into our nation and our children," the "electronic crack cocaine" of television and video games that he claims are "truly addictive." He's riding a bandwagon. Columbine turned it into a victory parade. Three days after Eric Harris and Dylan Klebold murdered thirteen of their schoolmates and then killed themselves,[1] President Bill Clinton cited Grossman by name and endorsed Grossman's video-games-teach-kids-to-kill thesis in his weekly radio address. The Republicans have known since their log cabin days that the media are evil, but after Columbine, even Democrats like Connecticut's Joe Lieberman signed on. The American Medical Association, the American Psychological Association, the American Academy of Pediatrics, the Surgeon General and other prestigious institutions have all endorsed the theory that violent media

---

1. The incident occurred on April 20, 1999, at Columbine High School in Littleton, Colorado.

make kids violent. It's a solid cultural consensus.

Grossman speaks to hundreds of organizations every year, from schools and colleges to Rotary Clubs, police departments and veterans' groups. He's an effective speaker and polemicist. "We live in the most violent era in peacetime human history," he sets up his audiences. If someone reminds him that the murder rate was eight times as high in medieval Europe as it is in modern America, that murder rates have been declining steadily in the Western world for the past five hundred years, he claims it's an illusion. "Medical technology saves ever more lives every year," he says. "If we had 1930s medical technology today, the murder rate would be ten times what it is." He claims that people are trying to kill people ten times as often as they used to do back when there were no police and no common access to courts of law, but that modern emergency medicine is masking the increase. . . .

A Fraudulent Theory

It's easy to believe that violence is getting worse: We hear about it all the time. It's easy to believe that mock violence in media is influencing behavior: What other violence do suburban kids see? Without question, popular culture is a lot more raucous than it used to be. It's a wild pageant, and it scares the culture police. But however many national leaders and prestigious institutions endorse the theory, it's a fraud. There's no evidence that mock violence in media makes people violent, and there's some evidence that it makes people more peaceful.

To start with, take a look at Col. Dave's claim about improved medical technology saving potential homicides. Of 1.5 million violent crimes in the U.S. in 1998, 17,000 were murders. Of the remaining number, according to the FBI, only 20,331 resulted in major injuries (the rest produced minor physical injuries or none at all). So if all the assault victims with major injuries had also died—improbable even with 1930's medicine—the 1998 U.S. murder rate would only have been double what it was—that is, would have been about 13 per 100,000 population rather than 6.3. But even 13 is well below the 23 per 100,000 murder rate of 13th-century England, the 45 per 100,000 of 15th-century Sweden, the 47 per 100,000 of 15th-century Amsterdam. We don't live in "the most violent era in peacetime human history"; we live in one of the least violent eras in peacetime human history.

Jib Fowles, a slight, handsome media scholar at the University of Houston at Clear Lake, worked his way through the media effects literature carefully and thoroughly when he was researching a book on the subject, mischievously titled *The Case for Television Violence*, which was published last year [1999]. Although Grossman and others are fond of claiming that there have been more than 2,500 studies showing a connection between violent media and aggressive behavior (the number actually refers to the entire bibliography of a major government report on the subject), the independent literature reviews Fowles consulted identified only between one and two hundred studies, the majority of them laboratory studies. Very few studies have looked at media effects in the real world, and even fewer have followed the development of children exposed to violent media over a period of years.

Media Violence an Excuse for Inaction

The continuing claims that media violence has proven adverse effects enables politicians to obscure known causes of violence, such as poverty and poor education, which they seem largely unwilling to address. Meanwhile, they distract the public with periodic displays of sanctimonious indignation at the entertainment industry, and predictable, largely symbolic demands for industry "self-regulation." The result is political paralysis.

Marjorie Heins, *Nation*, July 22, 2002.

In typical laboratory studies, researchers require a control group of children to watch a "neutral" segment of a television show while a test group watches a segment which includes what the researchers believe to be violent content—an actor or a cartoon character pretending to assault other actors or cartoon characters. Both segments are taken out of context, although sometimes the children watch entire shows. After this exposure, the researchers observe the children at play together or interacting with toys to see if they behave in ways the researchers consider aggressive. Aggression may mean merely verbal aggression, or rough play such as pushing and shoving, or hitting. Hitting is a rare outcome in these experiments; the usual outcome is verbal banter or rough play. Since the researchers, by the very act of showing the tapes, have implicitly endorsed the behavior they require the kids to watch, and further endorse the kids' response by standing around counting aggressive acts rather than expressing disapproval or intervening as a teacher or parent might do, the experimental arrangement is not exactly neutral.

Even so, the results of their laboratory experiments have been inconclusive. In some studies "aggression" increased following the "violent" television viewing; but in other studies the control kids who watched a neutral segment were more aggressive afterward. Sometimes kids acted up more after watching comedy. Boys usually acted up more than girls, but sometimes it was the other way around. "In the majority of cases," two investigators who reviewed a large number of laboratory studies found [according to Kenneth D. Gadow and Joyce Sprafkin], "there was an increase in negative behaviors in the postviewing interval for both aggressive and non-aggressive television material." Contradictory results such as these prove, at best, no more than what everyone already knows: that watching movies or television can stir kids up. They certainly don't prove that watching television makes children violent. They don't prove anything about the real world, Fowles argues, because they're nothing like the real world. . . .

The sociologist Howard Becker categorizes media violence zealots like Dave Grossman, . . . former Vice President Dan Quayle and former U.S. Secretary of Education William Bennett as "moral entrepreneurs." Part of their hostility, Jib Fowles argues, is simple snobbery, although surveys reveal that the affluent and the highly-educated watch about as many hours of television every week as everybody else. A deeper reason for their hostility is fear of losing social control. Thinking about the role of modern mass communications in social control, Fowles realized that entertainment media have come to satisfy many of the needs that religion used to fulfill: giving people a common frame of reference, a common community with which to identify and a safe place within which to experience emotional release. "The mass media comprise a new social institution," he told me. "And not only is it new, but it seems to be eating into the traditional social institutions of religion, community, family and so on. All these institutions are shrinking with the exception of education and mass media. We're choosing to integrate ourselves in very different ways and largely through the mass media." It shouldn't be surprising, then, that the moral entrepreneurs—the guardians of the traditional institutions—have led the attack. Blaming the media for criminal violence is one campaign in an ongoing turf war.

Studies Finding Positive Results

Fowles was struck by the contrast between the negativity of the moral entrepreneurs and the immense popularity of entertainment media. That popularity in itself argued against negative effects and in favor of positive effects. The media scholar wondered if any social science studies had turned up positive responses to watching television, including violent television. After a thorough search of the literature he found several which did. They were hard to find; though they were first-rate studies, they were seldom referenced because they disputed the reigning paradigm that television is bad for you.

In one thorough and careful field study, a highly respected psychologist named Seymour Feshbach had controlled the television viewing of some 400 boys in three private boarding schools and four boys' homes for six weeks, limiting half the boys to programs high in violent content and the other half to nonaggressive programs. Trained observers judged aggression levels in the boys before and after the controlled viewing period. "No behavioral differences were reported for the adolescents in the private schools," Fowles summarizes Feshbach's findings, "but among the poorer, semidelinquent youths, those who had been watching the more violent shows were calmer than their peers on the blander viewing diet." Feshbach concluded that "exposure to aggressive content on television seems to reduce or control the expression of aggression in aggressive boys from relatively low socioeconomic backgrounds." When Fowles interviewed Feshbach about this impressive finding, Feshbach interpreted it to mean that fantasy served the cause of self-control. "Television fantasies," he told Fowles, "supplement a person's own imagination, and help him discharge pent-up aggression in the same way that dreams and other products of the imagination can do.". . .

Fowles found support for the idea that entertainment media serves for emotional release in the work of a predecessor media scholar, Gerhardt Wiebe, who was dean of Boston University's School of Public Communication. Wiebe proposed that the function of the entertainment media is to ease the stresses of socialization, defined as "the process by which an individual becomes a member of a given social group." Being socialized means being molded and changed—from a rebellious adolescent to a productive, conforming adult, from a self-directed private individual before and after work to a group-directed employee during working hours—and such transformation is stressful. Television and other entertainment media work to relieve that stress. "All kinds of Americans," Fowles writes in his 1992 book *Why Viewers Watch*, "in all states of mind, turn to the medium for the balm it provides. The most troubled are perhaps the most aided. For the segment of the population that has been crushed by the real world, and has had to be removed from it, television is clearly a boon. Anyone who has visited an institution where humans are confined knows that television exerts a calming, beneficent influence. The administrators of hospitals, prisons and asylums realize that their charges can be highly volatile or depressed, and that television is an efficient, nonchemical means for easing their torments."

Media Messages

Wiebe defined three kinds of messages that media send. *Directive* messages come from authority figures and "command, exhort, instruct, persuade." Directive messages seldom get through, Wiebe observes; since the people at home control the remote, they tend to switch channels or downgrade directives into *maintenance* messages—the routine communications which support the knowledge and beliefs people already have. Thus programs on specialized subjects— Greece, say, or transvestite culture, or World War II—tend to draw audiences who already know about those subjects rather than the uninformed.

The primary function of the entertainment media, Wiebe proposes, is to supply *restorative* messages, which allow people to restore themselves "from the strain of adapting, the weariness of conforming." Restorative messages are "the adult counterpart of youthful protest and retaliation against authority figures" which appear "spontaneously, and apparently inevitably, as an antidote for the strictures of organized living." Restorative messages feature "crime, violence, disrespect for authority, sudden and unearned wealth, sexual indiscretion, freedom from social restraints." Their themes, Wiebe observes brilliantly, "seem to make up a composite reciprocal [that is, a negative counterset, an antidote] of the values stressed in adult socialization." Rock music, rap, movies like *Natural Born Killers* or *Pulp Fiction*, lurid music videos, video games and any number of "violent" television programs are evidence in support of Wiebe's insight. . . .

Media performances serve vicariously to intensify and then resolve tension, carrying away in the process all sorts of psychic detritus. They make it possible to put on a hero's armor, slay dragons and then hang up your armor and be yourself. Fowles calls the procedure "mental cleansing and redemption." At their most basic, entertainment media take the psychic garbage out.

The whole thrust of socialization across the past thousand years in Western culture has been toward reducing private violence in order to foster more effective social interaction in an increasingly complex and interdependent society. This movement, which historian Norbert Elias calls "the civilizing process," has advanced by internalizing the social prohibition against violence, and with that prohibition has come an advancing threshold of revulsion against violence. People who are seriously violent take pleasure in their violence. As people moved away from malevolence toward civility, the pleasure of doing violence was gradually displaced by the pleasure of seeing violence done—such as watching public executions and attending cockfights, bullfights and bareknuckle boxing matches.

The pleasure of seeing violence done has in turn gradually

been displaced by today's pleasure in seeing *mock* violence done in sports and in entertainment. Thus the increasing revulsion against bullfighting, hunting and boxing and the interdiction of public executions. More recently even mock violence has come under suspicion, especially as fare for children (who used to be taken to see public executions to show them why they shouldn't misbehave). So media violence has come to be tolerated more than endorsed. When real violence breaks out—the rise of juvenile delinquency in the 1950s, the riots and assassinations of the 1960s, the rash of white-on-white school shootings in the later 1990s—revulsion at media violence intensifies, and the mandarins of psychology and sociology trot out their statistical charts.

But there is no good evidence that taking pleasure from seeing mock violence leads to violent behavior, and there is some evidence, as Jib Fowles found, that it leads away. Bottom line: To become violent, people have to have experience with real violence. Period. No amount of imitation violence can provide that experience. Period. At the same time, mock violence can and does satisfy the considerable need to experience strong emotion that people, including children, build up from hour to hour and day to day while functioning in the complex and frustrating interdependencies of modern civilization. So can comedy; so can serious drama; but young males especially (and even not-so-young males) evidently take special satisfaction in watching mock violence, whether dramatic or athletic. "Whatever the relation of this need may be to other, more elementary needs such as hunger, thirst, and sex," concludes Norbert Elias, "one may well find that the neglect of paying attention to this need is one of the main gaps in present approaches to problems of mental health."

One Teen's View

A New Jersey teenager, Joe Stavitsky, responded to an attack on video games in *Harper's* magazine after Columbine with an eloquent letter in their defense. "As a 'geek,'" Stavitsky wrote, "I can tell you that none of us play video games to learn how (or why) to shoot people. For us, video games do not cause violence; they prevent it. We see games as a perfectly safe release from a physically violent reaction to the daily abuse leveled at us." Stavitsky, whose family emigrated from Leningrad when he was four to escape a communist dictatorship, concluded his letter with some pointed advice to the moral entrepreneurs. "The so-called experts should put away their pens," he advised, "and spend more time with their children or grandchildren, or better yet, adopt a child who has no home or family. Because there's only one sure way to prevent youth violence, and that is by taking care of youth." We do not take care of youth when we deny them entertainment which allows them to safely challenge the powerlessness they feel at not yet controlling their own lives and then to find symbolic resolution. Entertainment media are therapeutic, not toxic. That's what the evidence shows. Cyber bullets don't kill.

"Polls can interfere with the formation of public opinion."

Media Polls Negatively Affect the American Political Process

Ramesh Ponnuru

Much of the media's coverage of political elections and other events in recent years has become increasingly dominated by the practice of public opinion polling. This development has been condemned by some media critics. The following viewpoint by Ramesh Ponnuru is taken from a review of *Mobocracy: How the Media's Obsession with Polling Twists the News, Alters Elections, and Undermines Democracy* by political scientist Matthew Robinson. Ponnuru expresses agreement with the book's basic thesis that the American public is being ill-served by media polls that are often biased and inexpertly constructed and reported on. Ponnuru argues that polls create an illusion of certainty that belies the reality that most Americans do not have well-formed and informed opinions about many polling issues. Ponnuru is a senior editor for the conservative magazine *National Review*.

As you read, consider the following questions:
1. How does a poll's wording affect its results, according to Ponnuru?
2. Why do reporters rely on polls, according to the author?
3. How can polls interfere with the formation of public opinion, according to Ponnuru?

Ramesh Ponnuru, "Margin of Error," *National Review*, vol. 54, May 6, 2002, p. 49. Copyright © 2002 by National Review, Inc., 215 Lexington Ave., New York, NY 10016. Reproduced by permission.

P olls can provide useful information, but only if readers understand their limitations. The caveat is increasingly important as the media take polls with increasing frequency and decreasing quality. Where reporters once used polls in their stories, the polls now often make headlines themselves. But reporters rarely provide the information necessary to weigh the worth of poll results.

That failure and its consequences are the subject of Matthew Robinson's book.[1] The problem he identifies is not merely the ubiquity of polling, but what happens when bad polls combine with sloppy or biased reporting.

Biased Reporting

In early 2001, for example, several media outlets reported that a *Newsweek* poll had found that a plurality (41 percent) of the public thought the Senate should reject John Ashcroft's nomination as attorney general. Few of these outlets reported how *Newsweek* had reached this conclusion: by asking respondents, "Do you think Congress should approve [President George W.] Bush's choice of John Ashcroft for Attorney General, or reject Ashcroft as too far to the right on issues like abortion, drugs, and gun control to be an effective Attorney General?" It was a loaded question. Only the charge against Ashcroft was provided. When ABC ran a poll mentioning only that Bush had nominated Ashcroft, it found 54 percent support for his confirmation. A poll is only as good as its wording.

Readers also need to know the order in which the questions were asked. An unbiased question can get skewed results if the previous question was loaded. It's also important to know who was polled. When Al Gore picked Joe Lieberman as his running mate [in the 2000 presidential election], George W. Bush's lead over him dropped from 17 points to 2 points in one day. But the shift was illusory. Gallup had switched from questioning only "likely voters" in the 17-point poll to questioning "registered voters." Among registered voters, Republicans are more likely to vote than Dem-

---

1. *Mobocracy: How the Media's Obsession with Polling Twists the News, Alters Elections, and Undermines Democracy.* Roseville, CA: Prima, 2002.

ocrats; hence the discrepancy. Within a week, a Gallup poll confirmed that even post-Lieberman, Bush had a 16-point lead among likely voters. . . .

The Lewinsky scandal[2] was a milestone for polling—had the polls gone against [President Bill] Clinton, he might well have been removed. The poll results, in turn, were affected by the media's decision to ask the public whether Clinton should be removed from office, rather than whether [independent counsel Kenneth] Starr should submit a report, whether the House Judiciary Committee should hold hearings, etc. During Watergate,[3] the polls mainly stuck to the next stage of the process, allowing public support for Nixon's impeachment to build up slowly.

An Illusion of Certainty

Reporters lean on polls because they provide the illusion of numerical certainty amid all the spin. In political campaigns, reporters are torn between the conflicting desires to stay with the herd and to write a new story: Changes in the poll numbers provide the pivot point that lets everyone know when to make the switch together. Now the candidate whose campaign was brilliant last week is revealed as a sad-sack loser. His initiative on health care has bombed. How do we know that? Because he's down in the polls. Why is he down in the polls? Because his health-care initiative has bombed.

The overreliance on polls has the effect of overestimating public support for small policies that seem innocuous to voters. But it kills big ideas in the crib. Voters' initial reaction to any sweeping change is likely to be negative, so the first polls on it will show that it is unpopular. From then on, the idea can be dismissed as such. Polls can interfere with the formation of public opinion.

They can also create the illusion that public opinion exists when it does not. Reports that discuss what the public thinks about stem-cell research, or the Middle East peace process, are pointless because the public has no coherent, consoli-

2. President Bill Clinton was impeached by the House of Representatives in 1998 because of a political scandal relating to an affair with White House intern Monica Lewinsky; the Senate ultimately voted not to remove him from office. 3. the political scandal that drove President Richard Nixon from office in 1974

Manufactured News

Pollsters may wrap their findings in the authoritative language of social science, but that doesn't change the fact that a horse-race poll is still nothing more than manufactured news. The first newspapers to publish polls nearly two centuries ago called them "straw polls," named after the practice of throwing straw into the air to see which way the wind was blowing. Perhaps not much has changed after all. . . .

So why do credible journalists keep using these horse-race polls? A major reason is that news organizations have spent hundreds of thousands of dollars on their polls, and they have a proprietary interest in hyping the findings and reporting them as news.

Needless to say, the reason they spend so much on these polls is because they know that horse-race results bring in the readers and viewers. That polls are not news seems not to matter because polls add excitement and immediacy to the news. It's yet another subtle manifestation of the way bottom-line values drive the news these days.

Leonard Steinhorn, *Insight on the News*, December 25, 2000.

dated view on these matters, at least at the level of specificity needed to guide action. Polls, and media summaries of them, routinely gloss over the vast public ignorance and apathy that makes them so fluid.

Robinson does not shy away from this point. He writes that the reason poll results vary so widely—based on minor changes in wording—is that most people haven't given the issue in question much thought. They may tell a pollster that education is the top issue facing the nation, and the candidates may spend all their time talking about it as a result. But very few people will pay sufficient attention to know where the candidates stand on education.

Robinson may judge the voters a little too harshly: While it would be nice if they knew more about their government, some disengagement is inevitable and not irrational. (Modern government does too much for anyone to keep track of it all.) Moreover, given the dimensions of the problem that the author identifies, his proposed reforms are inadequate. Robinson wants the media to cover issues rather than polls, and for pollsters to force respondents to make trade-offs among competing goods rather than let them declare support for all nice-sounding things. But wouldn't either step increase the scope for political bias?

Our Political Culture

Robinson's case is, however, sound in its essentials. He has used the subject of the media and polls as a window on what's wrong with our political culture—and produced a contemporary brief for the representative and deliberative democracy the Founders wisely sought. If we have departed from their plan, the fault lies not in our polls but in ourselves.

| *"Academic people do research and they report the results. That is the basic argument for polls."*

Media Polls Positively Affect the American Political Process

Maurice Carroll

Maurice Carroll, a former political reporter for the *New York Times*, is director of the Quinnipiac University Polling Institute in Hamden, Connecticut. In the following viewpoint he defends the use of opinion polls, including election polls, even though polling may sometimes influence election results. Polling is simply a tool journalists use to gain information, he asserts, and the media have an obligation to provide that information to the public. Although polls may have potential drawbacks, such as discouraging people from voting, they still perform a valuable function in a democratic society, Carroll concludes.

As you read, consider the following questions:

1. What complaint did a senatorial candidate make about polls, according to Carroll?
2. What are some of the potential downsides of polls, according to the author?
3. How does Carroll respond to the argument that polling might make news or change election results?

W hen a Quinnipiac University poll reported that former governor James Florio of New Jersey was going
to be blown away in his attempt to win a U.S. Senate nomination in the Democratic primary this year [2000], two
things happened. First, contributions to Florio's campaign
dried up. Still unpopular from raising taxes while governor—
an act that cost him reelection—Florio already was in trouble. He was on his way to being inundated by the money that
multimillionaire Jon S. Corzine was spending on his own
campaign. But our poll made it worse. Second, Florio went
ballistic: Quinnipiac was a lousy poll, he said; we didn't know
New Jersey and we were sandbagging him.

Well, we were right. Corzine eradicated him—and was
well on the way to spending more money—$60 million—
than any Senate candidate in history.

But Florio was right, too. Our gloom-laden poll numbers
did in fact hurt him.

So, should we have kept quiet? . . .

The New Jersey Case

Let's look back at why Quinnipiac stuck its two cents into
the New Jersey election.

"We regularly poll New York, New Jersey and Connecticut," our poll director, Douglas Schwartz, explained at a
New York forum held by the American Association of Public Opinion Researchers. So how could we justify ignoring
the biggest race in the state? Besides, none of the other polls
that usually look at New Jersey were touching it. Without
us, the news media would have been dependent on those
old-fashioned, street-corner interviews or, worse yet, on information leaked by the competing campaigns.

So we knew it was hazardous to poll the primaries (who's
likely to vote?). We also knew that New Jersey was the pollsters' graveyard (55 percent of New Jersey voters in the state
are registered independent for both the primaries and general election) and we knew that voters have a habit of making
up their minds in the final minutes, but we plunged ahead.

As it turned out, we were right in the Corzine-Florio
Democratic primary—and also when we forecasted that the
Corzine–Bob Franks general-election race was too close to

call. Corzine and his multimillions of dollars won the election by a couple of points.

But it would be silly to suggest that what we reported didn't have an impact. Our early poll results hobbled Florio. Our later poll results motivated Corzine to unleash a few more election-day millions for his get-out-the-vote operation.

An Obligation to the Public

The question becomes: Should we, aware of the probable impact, have avoided reporting what we found—or should we have fudged the results in some fashion?

When the *New York Times*, where I was working as a political reporter, first debated using political polls in the 1970s, I demanded, "Why pay for polls? Pay your political reporters more money and we'll report what's going on."

My colleague, Frank Lynn, who was more perceptive than me, responded, "Look, the politicians have this information. Their pollsters report to them. So, if we're reporting about people who know more about what we're reporting than we do, we're not doing a good job."

Lynn was right. So the *Times* started using polls.

And the explanation of why we wrote in the paper about the stuff that we learned was simple: If the media know something, they have an obligation to let the public in on it. It's true, too, of universities such as Quinnipiac.

Academic people do research and they report the results. That is the basic argument for polls. If they're accurate, and most of the pre-election polls around the nation were remarkably accurate, it would be nonsensical to keep the information to yourself.

The Downside of Polls

Certainly, however, there is a downside. Polls might discourage would-be voters from actually bothering to cast a ballot on Election Day or persuade them that the election is in the bag for one candidate or the other so that they might as well do something else on Election Day. . . .

Polls might produce so much information, so early, so relentlessly, that citizens get bored and watch *I Love Lucy* reruns when responsibility says they should be watching the presidential debates. All that information might get in the way of real knowledge.

Polls might—no, they certainly do—make elections look like a game. Citizens who are supposed to be involved start to think of themselves as spectators.

Polls and Democracy

I argue that the public *should* respond to polls. They should do so for reasons that have to do with democracy—but not democracy in the knee-jerk sense that political leaders should be devoted to doing what public wants. There is ample room and a role for *both* leadership and responsiveness. Polls, in principle, can be stunningly democratic and especially egalitarian in that they *can attempt* to solicit opinion from a sample of *everyone*, not just those who have opportunities and an economic or other interest in being engaged actively in politics. In practice, of course, there are problems in pursuing such equality of voice, but polls can strive toward that goal and any other one. . . . It is important for this voice to be heard in the political process through reporting about public opinion in the press.

Bob Shapiro, plenary session at American Association for Public Opinion Research (AAPOR) conference, 2003.

Finally, and most insidiously, I think, polls intensify the tendency to look on society as a collection of groups instead of, as the Constitution wants us to behave, like a collection of individuals. A poll has to deal with demographic groups. Politicians have been calculating that way forever. But it's unhealthy if we start seeing ourselves like that.

Information a Valuable Commodity

When I was a young reporter, the editors used to tell us about the old-time reporters who would call this or that party chairman and accurately predict what would happen in an election. That technique has changed over the years. Most of the county chairmen today probably don't know anymore, and the reporters who were in their confidence— and also had the savvy to understand what they were told— are long gone.

But the sort of information that was gleaned in that way remains a valuable commodity, and the way that it is gathered now is through polling. And there's a simple check as to its accuracy. At Quinnipiac University, we poll all sorts of substantive governmental and political issues all year around and we're confident that our results are accurate. But there's one area of our polling that you can check on with ease: Were we right about an election or were we wrong? There's no room for interpretation or argument. Either we got it right or we didn't. And the way you see our accuracy in that poll should give you some indication of how accurate we are overall.

Poll director Schwartz had particular cause for pride when, in the [2000] New York race for the U.S. Senate between first lady Hillary Rodham Clinton and Rep. Rick Lazio, an election-eve poll showed Clinton ahead by 12 points. The other polls had the race much closer, and more than a few eyebrows were raised. Schwartz nailed it—Clinton won by 12 points.

That's an end result, of course. Pollsters report all along the way.

And if, as in the case of the Florio campaign, the information that we gather hurts a campaign, too bad. Not to sound overly noble, but the function of a pollster, the same as a news gatherer, is to seek out the truth, report it and let the chips scatter. I've always argued that it's wrong to calculate the impact of what you're reporting. . . .

When I went to work as a pollster, Quinnipiac University President John Lahey listed only one requirement: Do a responsible count and if that has some public impact, so be it.

That's what all responsible pollsters do. Quinnipiac, with an academic sponsor, simply packages its results and reports them to the news media. They can do what they want with what we tell them.

But when critics ruminate over the responsibility for results, I'm always reminded of a scene from one of my favorite movies, *Moonstruck*. Vincent Gardenia—playing the father, a mild sort of philanderer who has been discovered—is talking to his daughter about an affair that she's involved in.

"Always tell the truth," he counsels wearily. "They'll find out anyway."

So it is with polls. Do an honest job and, if it causes trouble—which it often will—that's too bad. One way or another, truth will win out.

"Millions of underage persons regularly absorb hundreds of millions of dollars in advertising for booze."

Alcohol Advertising Encourages Teens to Consume Alcohol

George A. Hacker

One of the areas of concern regarding the effects of media on society centers around advertisements for alcoholic beverages and whether they encourage alcohol abuse among the nation's youth. In the following viewpoint George A. Hacker argues that although alcohol marketers claim to adhere to voluntary industry standards against marketing to people under the legal drinking age, their advertising campaigns in fact reach millions of young people. The exposure of youth to media advertisements glamorizing alcohol consumption poses serious public health and safety concerns, he asserts. Hacker is the director for alcohol policies at the Center for Science in the Public Interest, a Washington, D.C., consumer advocacy organization that focuses on food and nutrition policies. He is also a coauthor of the books *The Booze Merchants* and *Marketing Booze to Blacks*.

As you read, consider the following questions:

1. How does Hacker respond to claims that youth are not direct targets of alcohol marketing?
2. How do alcohol advertisers use sporting events to promote their products, according to the author?
3. What point does Hacker make comparing tobacco and alcohol advertising?

Alcohol marketers say they have voluntary standards that prevent them from targeting consumers younger than the legal purchase age. They claim to avoid pitches that primarily appeal to teenagers and to pass up ad placements that reach an audience that is predominantly underage. Yet, we are told, when one reaches 21, former teens become potentially valuable alcohol consumers and legitimate targets for aggressive promotions to drink. The sad reality is that people under 21 are also in industry's cross-hairs; whether they're the intended targets is a matter of debate. The result, however, is the same. Millions of underage persons regularly absorb hundreds of millions of dollars in advertising for booze. Those messages weave through all media and countless marketing arenas; they mirror youth culture and relate directly to the interests, motivations, and aspirations of young people.

Much has been said about the content of ads; about their use of animals, cartoons, humor, music, athletics, and themes of belonging and friendship. Obviously, those elements catch the fancy of young people. One need only recall the Bud frogs and lizards, Spuds MacKenzie, and Whassup space-alien dogs to recognize the prominence of beer advertising in youth culture.

Strangely, those commercials comply with beer industry and broadcasters' advertising codes and meet (essentially meaningless) federal requirements. The Beer Institute's Voluntary Advertising Code asks whether the ads appeal primarily to underage people. . . . In 1999, even the Federal Trade Commission questioned the adequacy of those guidelines, suggesting that they be strengthened. No answer yet from the beer industry, which mistakenly interpreted that report as awarding brewers a gold star for responsibility.

Recently [December 2001], as a sop for accepting liquor ads after 50 years of restraint, NBC set a voluntary standard requiring that the ads run after 9 P.M. and audiences for those ads be at least 85% adult. Without suggesting an absolute limit on the number of underage persons in the audience, that's hardly an improvement. This week [in January 2002], *Advertising Age* magazine reported that all but one prime time show on NBC met that standard. Think about this possibility: an NBC show watched by everyone in

America over the age of 10. Nearly every single 10- to 19-year-old could be watching and that show would still meet the guideline. Obviously, rules such as these don't so much protect our children as serve them up to alcoholic-beverage advertisers such as Smirnoff Vodka. (For example, some 20% to 25% of the mammoth audience for the Super Bowl—the yearly showcase for funny, provocative, trend-setting, youth-oriented beer ads—is younger than 21. Those more than 30 million young people watching comprise as many as 40% of all the people under 21 in America.)

NBC's new "responsible" advertising standards, which apply to liquor products only, don't go far enough. And who knows how long they'll even last. Once liquor producers gain enough economic clout over NBC and other TV networks to demand the same treatment as beer, they're likely to erode or disappear entirely. Once those standards go, we shouldn't be surprised to see broadcast versions of liquor ads that now appear in youth-oriented magazines, such as *Vibe*, *Spin*, and *Rolling Stone*. Already, Jack Daniels whiskey is pushing for commercial time on NFL football, and Smirnoff Ice, a liquor-branded malt beverage, has its sights set on the Super Bowl. The Bacardi bat symbol formed the prominent backdrop for the rap half-time show at the [2002] Orange Bowl, where much of the collegiate audience (both in the stadium and at home) must have been underage.

Television provides but one example of industry's cavalier or deliberate targeting of young people. The United States Ski and Snowboard Association holds competitions all over the country; many of its members—and many of the contestants—are teenagers. Yet, this Vermont event last year [2001] provided a staging center for Captain Morgan and his Seagram rum. A look-alike was there glad-handing youngsters, and his likeness—in the form of a 10-foot-tall inflatable—was out on the race course; the contestants wore official Captain Morgan bibs. Until an outraged mother complained, the USSA's website also prominently featured the Captain and the product's logo; that site, a prime source of race information, attracts thousands of underage competitors and sports fans.

Lisa Leslie, Olympian and professional basketball player

and 2001 Sportswoman of the Year, [is] a clear draw for young people. No one doubts that Nike seeks young consumers and therefore invests in the WNBA; shouldn't we question though when Anheuser-Busch, whose Bud Light beer sponsors the league and hires Ms. Leslie to appear in its ads, does the same?

Beer companies plaster their names wherever sports audiences are found, and aim to take center stage as well: judging by the team's uniforms, you wouldn't know that San Diego's indoor professional soccer team is called the Sockers. . . .

Targeting Youth

Alcohol advertisers, in spite of what they say, have to target youth. As any advertiser knows, a major goal is to establish brand loyalty before your competitors do. By creating loyal customers out of kids, advertising produces two benefits: defeating the competition and producing more years of return for the advertising investment.

Consequently, there is no mystery involved when we realize that beer commercials are very youth-oriented. Beer commercials overwhelmingly link drinking with activities very popular with kids—volleyball, skiing, dancing, partying, etc. They also connect drinking with the emotional "hot buttons" for kids—popularity, sociability, physical attractiveness, adventure and romance. Not surprisingly, in a recent survey 16-year-olds listed beer commercials among their favorites.

David Walsh, *Washington Post*, July 11, 1997.

NBC, which will broadcast the [2002] Utah winter Olympic games, recently revitalized its on-air promotions, adding a techno beat and a blitz of images: crashing skiers, somersaulting freestylers, and careening hockey players, in an effort to appeal to today's high-tech, media savvy, stimulation-saturated youth. Extreme sports have been added to the games to broaden the audience and bolster the important youth market, including 18- to 21-year-olds. NBC said it wanted to talk to younger fans "as best we could." Anheuser-Busch, a prime sponsor of the games and a prominent advertiser during the events, will also be talking to the same crowd, as best it can.

NBC president and chief operating officer for the Olympics,

Randy Falco (who also presided over NBC's December [2001] decision to take liquor ads) says "[the] Winter Games in particular are really all about speed, all about edge. It's really perfect for a younger demographic."

Booze marketers also appeal to young people by developing familiar, sweet-tasting products. That's happening now in the "alcopop" market, where brewers are falling over themselves—and falling in with liquor companies too—to roll out hard lemonade and other fruit-flavored concoctions that resemble familiar soft drinks—in taste and often in looks—more than they do alcoholic beverages. Kids tell us that they go down easy and help introduce young people to other alcoholic drinks. National polls that we conducted last April [2001] found that teenagers know about "alcopops" a lot more than adults do, and they actually use them more.

Industry data, too, reflect the significant participation of underage users among consumers: Mintel International, as reported by Super Market Research, estimates that "nearly one-quarter of people age 19 to 20 drink coolers including spirits-based pre-mixed beverages, accounting for 7 percent of all cooler drinkers." And they're not even counting a lot of 15- to 18-year-olds! Mintel's calculation also fails to acknowledge that underage drinkers probably consume more than their proportional share of the products. Quite possibly, teenagers down some 10% of all the "alcopops" sold, if not more.

Policy makers accept as dogma the allegations that the tobacco industry reaches and targets young people. And, even though the scientific evidence is no more conclusive than that for the effects of alcohol ads, we accept as an article of faith that tobacco ads entice young people to take up smoking and keep on puffing. Why then does industry's argument—that advertising promotes brand identification and choice but does not encourage or increase alcohol use—get so much credit? In its propaganda, industry denies the effects of alcohol ads on young people, stressing the inconclusiveness of studies and citing dated edicts from the Federal Trade Commission and other studies from free-market oriented researchers.

The reality is different. The most recent pronouncements

of the FTC on the effects of advertising support common sense. In its 1999 report on the booze industry's voluntary advertising standards, the FTC determined (as had previous Chairman Janet Steiger in her 1991 testimony to Congress) that the inconclusive nature of the studies "does not rule out the existence of a clinically important effect of advertising on youth drinking decisions."

As recently as last June [2001], the United States Supreme Court struck down a Massachusetts ban on billboard advertising for tobacco products, but reaffirmed what common sense tells us about advertising. In ruling that the state met its burden of providing sufficient evidence of the relationship between tobacco advertising and smoking, the Court upheld its long-standing acknowledgment that product advertising stimulates demand and the absence of it suppresses it. Are we to believe that billboard advertising for tobacco products affects children, but frogs, lizards, party scenes, and humor in television ads for beer are impotent to do the same?

When it comes to assessing whether industry promotions, including advertising, influence our children to drink, we should trust our eyes and ears and our understanding of the effects of multi-million dollar advertising budgets. Whether alcohol producers intentionally target 15- and 16-year-olds is irrelevant. That they reach them with the most sophisticated means and the most seductive messages creates enough of a problem. We owe it to our children and to the public health and safety of America to challenge such marketing activities.

| "*Research from around the world has repeatedly demonstrated . . . that alcohol advertising . . . doesn't contribute to alcohol abuse.*"

Alcohol Advertising Does Not Encourage Teens to Consume Alcohol

David J. Hanson

The following viewpoint by sociologist David J. Hanson was inspired by hearings held by the New York state legislature on alcohol advertising, which aimed to determine whether such advertising has an effect on youth drinking. Hanson asserts that there is no scientific evidence demonstrating that advertisements encourage alcohol consumption or alcohol abuse by teenagers. He criticizes advocates of alcohol advertising bans for relying on "junk science" to support their arguments. Hanson is a sociology professor at the State University of New York at Potsdam and the author of *Alcohol Education: What We Must Do.*

As you read, consider the following questions:

1. To whom does Hanson compare critics of alcohol advertising?
2. What distinction does the author make between correlation and causation?
3. How do alcohol advertising critics misuse language, according to Hanson?

The New York State Assembly's Committee on Alcoholism and Drug Abuse recently [October 2002] held hearings on whether or not alcohol advertising has an effect on youthful drinking and, if so, what action the Assembly should take.

An Article of Faith

For most who testified, it was an article of faith: Alcohol ads cause young people to drink and strong action is needed. They converged on the hearing like the faithful assembling for a tent revival meeting. And their testimony was about as science-based as the rhetoric at a religious revival.

Research from around the world has repeatedly demonstrated for decades that alcohol advertising doesn't increase overall consumption, doesn't contribute to alcohol abuse, and doesn't cause non-drinkers to become drinkers. However, what it has found is that successful advertisers increase their market share at the expense of their competitors, who lose market share.

But scientific evidence was irrelevant to the true believers, who showed great faith in their beliefs. As one testified, "we should trust our eyes and ears" instead of believing what science has demonstrated.

Because those who opposed alcohol advertising were not supported by the scientific facts, they were forced to rely on anecdotal stories, emotional appeals, impressions, beliefs, and extensive use of "junk science." Of course there were testimonials, without which no tent meeting would be complete.

To "prove" that alcohol ads cause young people to drink, the faithful resorted to polls indicating that many people *think* alcohol ads increase youthful drinking. But polls also find that many people *think* that extraterrestrial aliens have landed on earth, that ghosts can communicate with us, and that some races are systematically inferior to others.

Meaningless Correlations

The true believers made great use of correlations that never, even once, proved anything. We know that increased consumption of ice cream is correlated with an increase in drownings. But that doesn't mean that eating ice cream causes people to drown. People are more likely to both eat ice cream and to go swimming (and sometimes drown) in warm weather.

Virtually every true believer used meaningless correlations to convince legislators to impose additional restrictions on advertising. Reflecting either naiveté or contempt for the Constitutionally guaranteed First Amendment free-speech rights of others, some even called for the prohibition of alcohol advertising.

Where Is the Science?

When I consider the pros and cons of alcohol advertising and its alleged effect on problem drinking, I find myself asking the crucial question: Where in the name of science is there proof that alcohol advertising is bad for society? Shouldn't there be some science to say it's so?

In 1996 I was asked to write a review for the *New England Journal of Medicine* on how advertising affects alcohol use. I did not find *any* studies that credibly connect advertising to increases in alcohol use (or abuse) or to young persons taking up drinking. The prevalence of reckless misinterpretation and misapplication of science allows advocacy groups and the media to stretch research findings to suit their preconceived positions.

Morris E. Chafetz, *Priorities*, vol. 9, no. 3, 1997.

The junk science congregation tended to have its own vocabulary, with meanings different from the "outside world." For example, much was made of alcohol ads appearing in youth-oriented magazines. To most people a youth-oriented magazine would have at least a majority of youthful readers. But to be clearly youth-oriented, perhaps the readership should be two-thirds young people, or perhaps three-fourths. Would you believe that anything above 15.8% youthful readership was defined as a youth-oriented magazine?!

This definition may be counter-intuitive, but if a common-sense definition were used the "researchers" wouldn't have any headline-grabbing findings to report. That's the nature of junk science. Those who practice it are interested in sound bites instead of sound science.

The misuse of language to persuade was pervasive. For

example, believers defined the term "binge" so loosely that a so-called binge drinker needn't have any measurable blood alcohol concentration (BAC). Similarly, 20-year-old married adults serving their country in the military would be "kids." Persuading others rather than presenting facts accurately is the goal of junk science.

No Scientific Evidence

The true believers had faith, deep conviction, emotional fervor and proselytizing zeal. What they didn't have was a shred of scientific evidence to support any of their beliefs and recommendations.

At the end of the day, the faithful returned home to the Center for Addiction and Substance Abuse, the Center for Science in the Public Interest, the Center on Alcohol Marketing and Youth, and other bastions of committed believers to refresh their zeal.

Periodical Bibliography

The following articles have been selected to supplement the diverse views presented in this chapter.

American Academy of Pediatrics	"Media Violence," *Pediatrics*, November 2001.
Craig A. Anderson and Brad J. Bushman	"The Effects of Media Violence on Society," *Science*, March 29, 2002.
Jonathan Durbin	"Fear Factory. Have the Media Overblown Canada's Health Scares?" *Maclean's*, June 9, 2003.
Marjorie Heins	"Screen Rage," *Nation*, July 22, 2002.
Terry Jones	"Media Accept Slanted Surveys," *St. Louis Journalism Review*, March 2003
Morgan Knull	"Slanted Polls Yield Biased News," *World & I*, October 2002.
Joan Konner	"The Case for Caution: This System Is Dangerously Flawed," *Public Opinion Quarterly*, Spring 2003.
Gerald F. Kreyche	"Excessive Awareness Is Driving Us Nuts," *USA Today*, November 2003.
Daphne Lavers	"The Verdict on Media Violence," *Insight on the News*, May 13, 2002.
Mary Muscari	"Media Violence: Advice for Parents," *Pediatric Nursing*, November/December 2002.
Public Health Reports	"Radio Daze: Young People Targeted by Alcohol Ads," July/August 2003.
Lori Robertson	"Poll Crazy," *American Journalism Review*, January/February 2003.
Joel Rosenbloom	"The 'Vast Wasteland' in Retrospect," *Federal Communications Law Journal*, May 2003
Henry Saffer	"Alcohol Advertising and Youth," *Journal of Studies on Alcohol*, March 2002.
Robert Samuelson	"The Limits of Media Power," *Newsweek*, October 6, 2003.

CHAPTER 4

How Will the Media Be Affected by the Internet?

Chapter Preface

Journalist and *New Yorker* writer A.J. Liebling is credited with the aphorism: "Freedom of the press is limited to those who own one." The quotation is frequently cited by those who argue that America's vaunted civil liberties, freedom of speech and freedom of press, are not as expansive as they seem. Anyone can speak from a soapbox or distribute leaflets, of course, but reaching and influencing a significant number of people requires owning a major newspaper or radio or television station—something that can cost millions of dollars. Thus freedom of the press, some argue, is a luxury only the wealthy can afford.

However, the advent of the Internet and the World Wide Web has changed this, according to some media scholars. For little to no cost, people can post their observations on websites that are potentially accessible to millions of computer users. In recent years hundreds of thousands of people have, in a sense, become press owners by creating their own personal websites or "blogs" (weblogs)—many of which are linked to each other. The September 11, 2001, terrorist attacks drew much attention to this phenomenon as people often found more compelling eyewitness accounts, reportage, and commentary about the attacks from personal websites than from television and newspaper reports.

Some people have wondered whether the Internet, with its multitude of blogs, will transform how the media operate. J.D. Lasica, editor of the *Online Journalism Review*, is one of several media observers who believe the Internet could undermine "the philosophical underpinnings of traditional media: We, the gatekeepers, gather the news and tell you what's important." In regards to both newspapers and television, media consumers are passive observers while reporters and editors decide what to cover, what stories to emphasize, and what the tone of coverage should be in their efforts to reach a target mass audience. But the rise of the Internet, Lasica goes on to argue, "blows away the top-down, one-to-many model that governs old media." Internet media consumers have greater control and power in creating content and in choosing what content to read. "On the Internet, control of the content, form and distribution of the message passes back and forth between publisher, user, and other participants."

The jury is still out on whether the Internet will give ordinary people the same power to influence exercised by a *New York Times* column or a CBS *60 Minutes* story. But most observers agree that, much as newspapers had to adjust to the arrival of radio and television, the traditional media will need to make adjustments in the Internet age. The viewpoints in this chapter examine various debates over how the Internet will affect modern mass media and communications.

"I don't turn to the papers much these days. For the most part, I rely on the internet to let me know what's happening."

The Internet Will Make Newspapers Obsolete

Neil Morton

Editor and journalist Neil Morton writes in the following viewpoint that while he grew up reading newspapers, he now gets most of his information from the Internet, and he asserts that many people in his generation and younger are doing the same. The various websites found on the Internet have much to offer that newspapers cannot match, including breaking news coverage, diverse opinions from around the world, and stories about topics of interest to young people. One important advantage of the Internet, he argues, is that it enables readers to choose and explore which stories are of most interest to them. Newspapers must radically change in order to survive ten or twenty years from now, he concludes. Morton was editor in chief of *Shift* magazine, a bimonthly Canadian publication that examined digital culture.

As you read, consider the following questions:

1. What were Morton's specific sources of information in his youth, compared to what he reads now?
2. What main tasks of newspapers are being done better on the Internet, according to the author?
3. What examples does Morton provide to support his claim that the Internet offers more than what newspapers provide?

Growing up in Peterborough, Ontario [Canada] (pop: 70,000), my parents, voracious readers, always had three newspapers delivered to their front door: the *Toronto Star*, the *Globe and Mail* (at the time, Canada's only national newspaper), and our local paper, *The Peterborough Examiner*.

This being the late eighties, meaning pre-web, the *Star* and *Globe* were my gateway to the outside world—to nearby Toronto, to Ontario, to Canada, to North America, to the rest of Planet Earth. My parents encouraged me to read them from cover to cover—"*Not* just the sports Neil!"—and I did, including the Op-Ed pages on occasion.

As for the *Examiner* . . . , it was my resource for local politics (the heated planning board sessions were always exhaustively covered), entertainment (anything from local theatre to barfights that escalated into assault causing bodily harm charges) and sports, including the Ontario Hockey League's Peterborough Petes (and hey, once in a blue moon, me scoring twelve points to lead my Adam Scott Lions' b-ball senior team to victory).

A Shift Away from Newspapers

Fast forward to 2002: My folks still turn to the papers as their primary source for news and analysis (they do go online, but it's primarily for email). Although I'll still buy a paper occasionally or grab one that's laying around the office (for Canadian news or a Canadian perspective on an international event), I don't turn to the papers much these days. For the most part, I rely on the internet to let me know what's happening out there.

The New York Times on the Web, Slashdot, USAToday.com, Google News Headlines, NewScientist.com, Technology Review, Salon, CNN.com, Wired News, BBC.co.uk, Guardian Unlimited, Slate, LaTimes.com, The Smoking Gun, PopBitch, Feed and Suck (when they were still alive and updating), the Onion, Modern Humorist and an assortment of weblogs (Metafilter, Fark, Plastic, Shift.com's Filter section)—that's where I get my daily dose of news, analysis and humour. I know many many others in their twenties, thirties and even forties who are in exactly the same boat.

So what does this all mean? Well, quite simply, it points

to a significant shift—one that has many newspaper publishers squirming—away from papers as we know them. I fall in between the old and new vanguard of media in that I was raised on newspapers and am now weaning myself on the web, so I'm loyal to both. But a new generation is growing up on the net and for many of them, the print papers aren't even an option; even if they do read the papers, they tend to end up on the online version (TheStar.com, not the *Toronto Star*) through a referral.

A Medium for the Masses

If they accept the new realities dictated by the Internet, the new journalists will be light years ahead of publishers and old-guard editors who continue to think within the box of mass media. Mass media are about reaching large audiences and target demographics. Mass media control the content, form and distribution of the message. Mass media serve each person's general interests while serving no individual's specific needs.

The Internet, however, is not a mass medium. It's a medium for the masses. The Net blows away the top-down, one-to-many model that governs old media. Instead, it encompasses one-to-one, one-to-many and many-to-many communication, with the individual firmly rooted at center stage. On the Internet, control of the content, form and distribution of the message passes back and forth between publisher, user and other participants. The user may adopt the mantle of reporter, editor and publisher, creating new forms of individualized content.

J.D. Lasica, *Online Journalism Review*, April 2, 2002.

Newspapers have always been in the business of reporting news, breaking news, analyzing news, but now that job is done adequately, and with much more immediacy, on the internet. For example, people flocked to the web in droves [when the September 11, 2001, terrorist attacks occurred] to learn everything they could about the disaster and to connect with others. Most of the print papers were light-years behind in their coverage of the biggest event of our generation—though some did put out special second editions that day, and of course their online versions were all over it.

Many 12- to 35-year-olds now view Salon and Slashdot as

seminal news sources, news sources their parents likely haven't even heard of. With the net, now *we* go and find the news; the news doesn't get selected for us by editors and writers. *We* go out and discuss various viewpoints on political events in threads and discussion boards rather than having them dictated to us by op-ed pages with their own agenda.

What the Web Offers

While many mainstream media outlets were feeding us their pro-U.S. version of the war in Afghanistan[1] and American foreign policy, we could find blogs like Metafilter and Plastic discussing the flip-side of the coin and linking to superb articles at places like the Guardian that were giving us the Bigger Picture (for example, that the number of civilian casualties in Afghanistan has now overtaken the lives lost on 9/11).

There are countless other examples of what the web offers us that the print papers don't: . . .

- When Orlando Magic star Grant Hill went down with yet another season-ending injury late [in 2001], hardcore basketball fans were able go online to get in-depth coverage of team—and community—reaction at OrlandoSentinel.com or ESPN.com.
- If you want to find an American perspective on Canadian issues, you can go to Plastic's "Canadians" category.
- The *Globe and Mail* has for years been anti-environment, or at least skeptical of any science that says something's wrong with our planet. On the web, through sites like Utne Web Watch or Grist Magazine, you can find plenty of evidence that not everyone is taking that narrow-minded pro-business, right-wing, conservative approach.
- If you want to see celebrity divorce petitions for the likes of Pamela Lee, Janet Jackson and Michael Jordan, you can go to SmokingGun.com.
- *The Peterborough Examiner* has a tiny section called the Odd Spot on their cover page, which points to a ludicrous news story. Many other papers have similar sec-

1. Following the terrorist attacks on New York City and Washington, D.C., in September 11, 2001, U.S. military forces entered Afghanistan and removed that nation's regime because it had been harboring the terrorist organization believed to be responsible for the attacks.

tions. On the net, however, there's a gigantic and wonderful 24/7 Odd Spot at Fark.

- Newspapers do a horrible job of covering videogames, now a mainstream phenomenon. On the internet, there are plenty of webzines like GameCritics.com, Joystick 101.org, RobotStreetGang.com and Womengamers. com that are covering their cultural impact.

As a kid, I didn't have the option to turn to other sources for other viewpoints or peripheral information. I pretty much took as gospel what our national newspaper was saying. I thought the *Globe* was giving me ninety-nine percent of the "news," but in truth, as I've discovered via the web, it's more like five to ten percent of what's really going on. If I had had the choice to go online, I would likely have gravitated toward the internet and away from the coffee-table, like so many teens and young adults are doing now.

As cliché as it sounds, the world is your oyster on the net in the way it can never be in newspapers, which, by no fault of their own, have been overtaken by technology in the way radio was by TV.

Newspapers Must Change or Perish

Over the next ten to twenty years—and this is a conservative estimate—newspapers will have to substantially re-invent themselves or they will perish. In some cases, maybe only the online version will exist; I already know many people— and this *has* to be considered a major concern among newspaper publishers—who used to buy or subscribe to a daily that now just check out the (free) online version. If the print version does survive, it will look much different—perhaps it will primarily be service-oriented, like a gigantic Life section or something.

Newspaper big-wigs are doing their strategizing behind closed doors, but they'll have to really have their thinking caps on. Soon, new wireless technologies will enable us to access the net whenever, wherever: in the kitchen, on the subway, on the toilet, at the cottage, in the car . . . , in the pool, at the laundromat, at the hairdresser, on the treadmill. If I have the choice between reading a big clunky paper that leaves my hands stained with black ink and a portable internet that offers insane amounts of legible news content and clean design, guess who's going to win out?

The web—still very much in its infancy but maturing rapidly as a new mass medium—is fast becoming the number one resource for news. It can disseminate information the way no other medium can. And that's where the next generation of Moms and Dads will be going with their morning cup of coffee.

"Newspapers will be around for many years to come."

The Internet Will Not Make Newspapers Obsolete

Mark Briggs

Some observers have predicted that daily newspapers will soon become obsolete in a time when people can get all their news from the Internet. In the following viewpoint Mark Briggs, an editor for the *Everett Herald*, a newspaper serving the northwest region of the state of Washington, disputes this conclusion in an article written in 2001 when the *Herald* was celebrating its hundred-year anniversary. Briggs, looking ahead to the next century, argues that while technology will certainly transform how newspapers will be made and distributed, their basic mission—delivering news and advertising to the customers in the communities they serve—will not change. Newspapers will still prove to be indispensable, he concludes.

As you read, consider the following questions:

1. How many newspapers does Briggs predict would be delivered daily in the United States in 2001?
2. What predictions does the author make about what newspapers will look like ten, twenty, and a hundred years from now?
3. How will the news be gathered and reported in the year 2101, according to Briggs?

Television was supposed to kill the radio and the Internet was supposed to kill newspapers, so what happened? Most people today get some news from all four media, proving that Americans have an apparently insatiable appetite for news. More than 50 million newspapers will be delivered in the United States daily in 2001.

The past 100 years have seen great advancement at *The Herald*, and in newspapering in the United States. As we take time on *The Herald's* 100th anniversary to look back, it's also worth a glance forward. We may not be able to accurately predict how (some would say if) newspapers will progress to the year 2101, but we do know *The Herald* and other newspapers will be around for many years to come.

A Newspaper's Core Mission

Technology will obviously be the greatest influence of change in newspapering in the future. But no technological advancement will change *The Herald's* core mission: delivering timely, relevant, interesting and important news and advertising to Snohomish and Island counties. It will be the delivery of that news and advertising, however, that is likely to change the most through new technology.

Here's a look at where *The Herald* and the business of newspapering will travel during the next 100 years.

In five years: Currently, most newspapers publish a Web site that closely mirrors the printed newspaper. In 2006, there will be more reliance among readers on electronically delivered news content than today [2001].

The good news for readers is that news publishers will respond to this need, publishing their news for all kinds of wireless, digital and portable devices. The bad news is that the day of free content on the Web—or anywhere else in the wireless world—will have ended.

Paying for Content

News consumers will pay for content they receive—on the Web, on a cellular phone, on a handheld computer—but that content will be specifically tailored to their needs and tastes. The number of copies printed by news publishers will diminish, but the number of people who read the news and advertising will continue to grow.

Newspapers, TV stations and radio stations will have jettisoned their single-purpose identities and transformed into broad-reaching news companies. Internet and satellite radio will be common in new cars, forever changing the radio broadcast game in the same manner the World Wide Web altered the content publishing world in the late 1990s.

For newspapers, this will mean a new opportunity: to reach people in their cars. Newspaper reporters will routinely file audio reports of the stories they write for the paper. Around here, people will listen to *The Herald* in their cars and at work. We'll bring the newspaper to life.

In 10 years: The profession of news reporting became much more efficient with telephones, tape recorders and computers over the years. In the year 2011, the tools for news gathering will make the advent of the Internet look like the Stone Age.

Instead of a steno notebook and a pen, reporters will use a handheld, digital, wireless computer that will record interviews, shoot photographs, work as a cellular phone and connect to the Internet. This will be part of a 24-hour publishing cycle that will connect news consumers to the news.

With reporters wirelessly connected, readers won't have to wait for the morning paper to find out who won a high school football game or how the jury decided a big case. The morning newspaper will continue to be a valued product, however, since the immediacy of news consumption will not usurp the desire for great depth in news coverage.

Changing Newsprint

In 20 years: Newsprint will evolve, finally, into a synthetically enhanced product that will look and feel just like the paper of the previous century. *The Herald* will install a new printing press that prints more efficiently on this new material.

The printing of newspapers will take only 20 percent of actual paper from trees. The rest will be manufactured out of a new-age plastic that is completely recyclable. To ensure the rate of recycling, *The Herald* will pick up old newspapers from subscribers' homes once a week, bringing the material back to the printing plant where the newspapers will be

The Web Will Not Replace Other Media

The web is quite different from other mass media, and it will not be a replacement for newspapers, radio, or television. The web is interactive, and thus it forces users to be active: enter, search, scroll, and click. A massive amount of information can be obtained quickly, but we must do a lot of work. Radio and television allow us to sit back and simply listen or watch. The web is most like a newspaper in asking us to make choices about what to focus our attention on, but newspapers organize the material much better, and they invite us to relax and read. By contrast, when we go to the web, we sit at attention and tend to skim or scan the screen, always ready to click on something different.

It will be easy for traditional media to successfully compete with the web if they emphasize what they do best: present an easy-going, well-ordered account of the world.

Eric Johnson, *Argus Leader*, January 2, 2000.

---

wiped clean and folded for reuse.

By cutting out the waste management companies in the recycling process, *The Herald* will dramatically increase the efficiency of the entire process. After years of electronic reader experiments that were supposed to doom the daily newspaper, subscriptions will increase dramatically with the introduction of this new synthetic "news-plastic."

A Century from Now

In 100 years: Will newspapers still exist in the year 2101? Yes, although you wouldn't recognize them today. Newsprint—and "news-plastic"—will be replaced by a reusable yet durable form of e-paper that will allow readers to "download" the new version of *The Herald* each morning as soon as they want it.

This e-paper will likely resemble today's newsprint: It will be flexible, foldable and very portable. Newspaper carriers will no longer go door-to-door each morning. Instead, they will deliver and service the electronic port machines that will receive and "print" the paper each morning. A subscription to *The Herald* will include this service.

The news will be gathered in fundamentally the same fashion, with professional reporters following leads, interviewing, researching and writing. It was essentially the same process in 1801, 1901 and today, in 2001, so there's no reason to think people won't desire well-reported, well-written and well-edited stories in 2101. The narrative story was with us long before newsprint, and it will remain with us long after.

Despite the challenges that newspapers have faced in recent years, including skyrocketing newsprint costs and massive mergers across the country, the newspaper is still the most respected source of news and information in the United States.

Will that ring true 100 years from now? Yes, but the process of printing the newspaper will change dramatically, and the ritual of walking out on the doorstep with a cup of coffee to pick up the morning paper will seem as antiquated as milk delivery on your doorstep seems today.

The year 2101 will be an even more wired world than the one we live in today, but *The Herald* will still be producing a product indispensable to those in and around Snohomish and Island counties.

"Sexual predators use the Internet to distribute child pornography."

The Internet Has Made Child Pornography a National Problem the Government Must Address

Part I: George W. Bush; Part II: Morality in Media

In the 1990s Congress passed several laws designed to protect children from being exposed to pornography on the Internet, only to have several of those laws overturned by the Supreme Court. The following two-part viewpoint makes the case that the national regulation of Internet pornography is both constitutional and desirable. Part I is taken from remarks by President George W. Bush at a gathering of law enforcement officials. Bush argues that the Internet is a powerful tool that has been abused by criminals seeking to harm children, and he calls for passage of new federal legislation against child pornography. Part II, taken from a news release by the organization Morality in Media, presents the results of a poll showing that most Americans support vigorous law enforcement of federal laws against Internet obscenity. Morality in Media works to curb traffic in illegal obscenity.

As you read, consider the following questions:
1. What would the federal legislation Bush supports accomplish, according to the president?
2. According to Morality in Media, what has the Supreme Court said about enforcing obscenity laws?

I

Thank you all for coming. Welcome to the White House. And thanks for the work that most of you do on behalf of protecting this country's children. Because children are so vulnerable, they need the constant protection of adults. And because children are so vulnerable, they're often the targets of cruel and ruthless criminals. . . .

I want to discuss with you several aggressive steps we are taking to protect our children from exploitation and from danger on the Internet. . . .

When a child's life or innocence is taken, a grave and unforgivable act has occurred. A parent's worst nightmare has become real. And you all here are on the front lines of this great struggle to see to it that no parent has to live through the nightmare. That's what you're doing.

Challenge of the Internet

The Internet is a remarkable technology. We've all learned that. It's revolutionized education, vastly increased the flow of information, increases our knowledge. We're now in closer touch with our family and friends. People are now connected across the globe. It's an exciting tool. But . . . more than half of the nation is now online, and 75 percent of the children are online.

The flow of information is freer and broader. Yet the new freedom presents us with an unprecedented challenge: A technology that brings knowledge also brings obscenity and danger. Until recently, the worst kind of pornography was mainly limited to red-light districts or restricted to adults or confined by geography, isolated by shame. With the Internet, pornography is now instantly available to any child who has a computer. And in the hands of the wrong people, in the hands of incredibly wicked people, the Internet is a tool that lures children into real danger.

Sexual predators use the Internet to distribute child pornography and obscenity. They use the Internet to engage in sexually explicit conversations. They use the Internet to lure children out of the safety of their homes into harm's way. Every day, millions of children log on to the Internet, and every day we learn more about the evil of the world that has crept into it. In a single year, one in four children between the ages of 10 and 17 is . . . involuntarily exposed to pornography. That's one in four children. One in five children receives a sexual solicitation over the Internet. One in 17 children is threatened or harassed. We've got a widespread problem, and we're going to deal with it.

We don't accept this kind of degrading. It's unacceptable to America. We don't accept offensive conduct like this in our schools, in the commercial establishments, and we can't accept it in our homes. We cannot allow this to happen to our children. The chief responsibility to protect America's children lies with their parents. . . .

There are several practical things parents can do to protect their children from the dangers of online predators. First of all, pay attention to your children. If you love your children, pay attention to them. Know what they're doing. Share your experience with your children. Make it clear to your children about the potential online dangers they face. Make it clear to them the kinds of websites they need to avoid.

Children need to be told to never provide personal information to anyone online. It seems like a simple parental responsibility. Mothers and dads all across America need to do their job and make it clear to their children there can be danger by providing personal information. Don't share any passwords—that's a logical thing for a mom or a dad to do, tell their children not to share a password with a total stranger. Don't agree to meet with somebody they've never met. Don't agree to meet with somebody that chats them up on the Internet, unless the mom or dad is with them. . . .

Parents have the first and foremost responsibility. Yet we as a society share this duty, as well, and that's what we were talking about today. Parents need allies in the upbringing of their children. Our nation should make the essential work of mothers and fathers easier, not harder. Our government, at every level, must take the side of responsible parents, and we will.

We're waging an aggressive nationwide effort to prevent the use of the Internet to sexually exploit and endanger children. . . . Through an FBI program called Innocent Images, we identify, we investigate, and we prosecute sexual predators across the country.

FBI agents are obtaining evidence of criminal Internet activity by conducting undercover operations, using fictitious screen names and entering into online chat rooms. . . .

Innocent Images prosecutions increased by more than 50 percent over the last two years [since 2000]. We're making progress. Just like we're hunting the terrorists down one at a time, we're hunting these predators down one at a time, too. Based on the progress, I'm pleased to announce that we will expand this program and significantly increase the funding in the next fiscal year [2003]. We will also seek to almost double funding for the Internet crimes against children task forces, from $6.5 million in fiscal year 2002 to $12.5 million in fiscal 2003. These task forces help state and local authorities enforce laws against child pornography and exploitation.

Since 1998, the task forces have helped train more than 1,500 prosecutors and 1,900 investigators. They've served 700 search warrants and 1,400 subpoenas. The task forces have provided direct, investigative assistance in more than 3,000 cases. They've arrested more than 1,400 suspects. These task forces are a great success. . . .

Federal Laws Needed

We're taking aggressive steps to protect children from exploitation and victimization. And the United States Congress can help by passing the Child Obscenity and Pornography Prevention Act. The House has passed this important bill, and I want to thank them for their good work.

The House passed a bill which makes it illegal for child pornographers to disseminate obscene, computer-generated images of children. It's an important piece of legislation. The Senate needs to act soon. [The Senate did not pass the bill in 2002.] The Senate needs to get moving and join the House in providing our prosecutors with the tools necessary to help shut down this obscenity, this crime—these crimes against children.

II

Eight out of ten Americans (81%) believe federal laws against Internet obscenity should be vigorously enforced, and seven out of ten (70%) believe that strongly. A higher percentage of women support vigorous enforcement of federal laws against Internet obscenity than men (90% versus 72%).

On the other hand, seven out of ten Americans (70%) say they do not believe these laws are currently being vigorously enforced.

Benson. © 1996 by United Feature Syndicate. Reproduced by permission.

The results come from a just-released opinion poll conducted by the Wirthlin Worldwide survey research company for Morality in Media. The national telephone poll of 1,004 Americans over age 18 was conducted from March 1st through 4th [2002] and has a margin of error of plus or minus 3.1 percentage points at a 95 percent confidence level.

One Person's Reaction

Morality in Media President Robert W. Peters commented: "Hardcore pornographers have been telling us for years that widespread availability of hardcore pornography is proof of community acceptance. Well, eight out of ten Americans saying that they want vigorous enforcement of federal laws against Internet obscenity adds up to community rejection of hardcore pornography, and support for prosecutors who vigorously enforce obscenity laws.

"Most Americans do not want their Internet-connected

nation and homes drowning in a floodtide of illegal hardcore pornography. They want to live and raise children in a decent society, and in the 1973 *Paris Adult Theatre* obscenity case, the Supreme Court said that there is a 'right of the Nation and of the States to maintain a decent society.'

"Two federal obscenity laws . . . were amended in 1996 to clarify that use of an interactive computer service to transmit obscene material is prohibited. Violations of these two statutes also constitute predicate crimes under the federal Racketeer Influenced and Corrupt Organizations (RICO) law . . . which, among other things, permits the forfeiture of an entire pornography empire.

"For nine long years, there has been little or no enforcement of federal obscenity laws against major commercial distributors of hardcore pornography. In the 2000 presidential elections both major party candidates expressed their support for enforcement of federal obscenity laws. Now is the time for the winner to begin fulfilling his important campaign pledge."

Poll Questions and Results

Those interviewed were told, "Since the World Wide Web became more accessible in 1995, more than 20 million Web sites have been created. A large number of these Internet Web sites contain hard-core pornography. The Supreme Court has said that those who distribute hard-core pornography can be prosecuted under obscenity laws. In 1996, Congress expanded the federal obscenity laws, making it a crime to distribute obscene materials on the Internet."

They were asked, "In your opinion, should the federal laws against Internet obscenity be vigorously enforced?" For all respondents, the results were:

- Yes, strongly: 70%
- Yes, somewhat: 12%
- No, somewhat: 9%
- No, strongly: 7%
- Don't know/refused: 2%

Support for obscenity law enforcement was particularly strong in the female demographics. Here are some percentages:

- Women, overall: 90%

- Women, 35–54: 92%
- Women, over 55: 94%
- Married women: 93%
- Homemakers: 93%
- Working women: 89%

Support was also strong among parents with children:

- Respondents married with children: 88%
- Respondents with 3 children: 90%
- Respondents with 4 or more children: 88%
- Working women with children: 91%

In the second question, respondents were asked, "Based on what you may know, do you believe the federal laws against Internet obscenity are currently being vigorously enforced?" For all respondents, the results were:

- Yes, strongly: 10%
- Yes, somewhat: 11%
- No, somewhat: 24%
- No, strongly: 46%
- Don't know/refused: 9%

"The law is too clumsy an instrument to regulate sexual expression on the Web."

The Internet Has Made Government Action Against Child Pornography Untenable

Jeffrey Rosen

In 1973 the Supreme Court established guidelines for obscenity laws that provided for the banning or regulation of materials if they were deemed patently offensive "by contemporary community standards." The proliferation of Internet pornography has raised questions about how the community standards test can be applied to online pornography. The following viewpoint by Jeffrey Rosen was written in response to a 2002 Supreme Court ruling on the 1998 Child Online Protection Act, a federal law that attempted to protect children from Internet pornography. Rosen argues that the Supreme Court's approach to pornography assumed a national consensus on what is or is not appropriate for teenagers and adults, but he contends that such an agreement no longer exists. Federal laws against pornography could undermine free speech on the Internet, he concludes. Rosen is a legal affairs writer for the *New Republic*, a journal of opinion.

As you read, consider the following questions:
1. How does the Child Online Protection Act define "material that is harmful to minors"?
2. How are the ideas about pornography expressed by the Supreme Court dated, according to the author?
3. What alternatives to federal legislation does Rosen suggest to cope with child pornography?

Jeffrey Rosen, "Minor Infraction—the Supreme Court Misunderstands Porn," *New Republic*, June 3, 2002, p. 17. Copyright © 2002 by The New Republic, Inc. Reproduced by permission.

Opponents of the Child Online Protection Act are putting their best face on [the] Supreme Court decision to send *Ashcroft v. ACLU* back to a lower court for further study.[1] The ACLU [American Civil Liberties Union] was thrilled when a Philadelphia district court, concerned that the law violated free speech, temporarily banned it in 1999. And Ann Beeson, the ACLU lawyer who argued the case before the Supreme Court, said the Court "clearly had enough doubts about this broad censorship law to leave in place the ban, which is an enormous relief to our clients."

But that's too rosy a reading of the Court's fractured opinions. In fact, the five-to-four decision suggests that a majority of justices have embraced the implausible claim that underlies the Child Online Protection Act and obscenity law more generally: that there is a national consensus about which sexually explicit materials are appropriate for teenagers as well as adults. But this consensus no longer exists. The 1950s-era consensus on obscenity to which the justices are clinging has been overtaken by the reality of America's viewing habits and sexual mores. And unless the Court abandons this archaic legal framework, which allows America's most conservative communities to impose their values on the rest of the nation, it could dramatically undermine free speech on the Internet.

The Child Online Protection Act

Passed in 1998, the Child Online Protection Act (COPA) defines "material that is harmful to minors" as any communication—including pictures, writings, or recordings—that, in the eyes of "the average person, applying contemporary community standards," is designed to "appeal to . . . the prurient interest"; "depicts . . . in a manner patently offensive with respect to minors, an actual or simulated sexual act or sexual contact, an actual or simulated normal or perverted sexual act, or a lewd exhibition of the genitals or post-pubescent female breast"; and "taken as a whole, lacks serious literary,

---

1. In May 2002, the Supreme Court sent the Child Online Protection Act of 1998 back to the United States Court of Appeals for the Third Circuit for reconsideration. In March 2003, the lower court declared the law unconstitutional—a decision that was appealed back to the Supreme Court.

artistic, political, or scientific value for minors." Under the law, any commercial website that posts this material must restrict access to minors under age 17 through the use of credit cards, adult access codes, or digital certificates—or risk prison terms of up to six months and civil fines of up to $50,000 per violation.

The problem is that while dial-a-porn operators and mail-order pornographers can deny their products to customers from states or localities that consider those products obscene, Web pornographers can't. To make sure customers from certain communities can't view their material, websites would have to restrict it for everyone.

That's why the Philadelphia court struck down COPA, holding that it would require "any material that might be deemed harmful by the most puritan of communities in any state" to be placed behind an age-verification screen. This, the appellate court recognized, would give adults on the Web free access only to material that America's most conservative communities considered fit for children.

But in his troubling opinion [in *Ashcroft v. ACLU*], Justice Clarence Thomas—joined by Justices William H. Rehnquist, Antonin Scalia, Sandra Day O'Connor, and Stephen Breyer—disagreed. The five justices announced that the possibility that juries in different regions might apply community standards differently wasn't, by itself, constitutionally problematic—even if it required websites to restrict access for everyone. In separate statements, Justices O'Connor and Breyer stressed that in passing COPA, Congress intended to adopt a national standard for identifying material harmful to minors on the Internet, even though different local juries might interpret it in different ways. "A nationally uniform adult-based standard," Breyer declared, "significantly alleviates any special need for First Amendment protection," by allowing national rather than local values to prevail. As long as the nation agreed on what was harmful to minors, Breyer suggested, the material could be restricted across the board.

With characteristic deference to Congress, Breyer assumed the House of Representatives and the Senate were correct when they announced that this national consensus exists. But the evidence from American viewers suggests otherwise. Consider soft-core "teasers"—free pictures from commercial pornographers—many of which are now available without adult verification and which Congress intended COPA to restrict. These are the equivalent of the soft-core girlie magazines that the Court in the 1960s said states could prohibit teenagers from buying unless they were age 18 or over. But it's hard to discern a national consensus that viewing soft-core porn is inappropriate for, or harmful to, 16-year-olds today. On mainstream television, naked breasts are no longer quarantined on late-night, public-access TV stations, as they were when I was a lad in the 1970s. Bare breasts and bottoms can be found on network shows like "NYPD Blue." Some of the most successful shows on HBO are sexual documentaries like "Real Sex," "Taxicab Confessions," and "g-String Divas," a graphic show about strippers. And millions of underage viewers are saturated with sexual images on MTV.

No National Consensus on Porn

The variety of state laws and jury verdicts on the subject of pornography also shows the absence of a national consensus. Among the 25 states that prohibit the display of material harmful to minors, some prohibit only fully exposed breasts; but a Wisconsin court recently upheld a conviction for exposing a child to a photograph of a woman with her "shirt and jacket open to the waist without exposing her nipples." Given this regional variation, the Supreme Court has long held that asking a jury to apply a national standard for "patently offensive" content outside of the TV-broadcast medium would be "an exercise in futility." At a time when our culture has never been more sexualized, it's hard to fathom why Breyer and O'Connor have now concluded otherwise.

Even more troubling, COPA isn't limited to pornographic images online: It encompasses written descriptions of actual or simulated sexual acts that some juries might consider harmful to minors. It's shocking that the federal government is trying to restrict access to text on the Internet—after all, the Supreme Court hasn't allowed the banning of books since the late 1940s. And yet only Justice John Paul Stevens voted to invalidate COPA on these grounds, emphasizing that "because communities differ widely in their attitudes toward sex, particularly when minors are concerned, the Court of Appeals was correct to conclude that . . . applying community standards to the Internet will restrict a substantial amount of protected speech that would not be considered harmful to minors in many communities."

But Stevens refused to follow his powerful reasoning to its logical conclusion: Namely, if there is no national consensus about what's obscene for children, there's also no national consensus about what's obscene for adults. This means that any application of federal obscenity statutes on the Web threatens to violate the First Amendment because all obscenity laws are based on the no-longer-credible assumption that people can agree on what's obscene. In his decision, however, Stevens clung to the idea that some kind of agreement about obscenity still exists. In a remarkable sentence, he wrote, "The kind of hard-core pornography involved in Hamling,[2] which I assume would be obscene under any community's standard, does not belong on the Internet."

Dated Notions of Pornography

This shows how removed even the most liberal justice is from the reality of pornography on the Internet today. The hard-core pornography involved in the *Hamling* case was the kind of material that might have been considered obscene in 1974—the year before Stevens, now 82, was appointed to the Court. The case involved a successful attempt to suppress a satiric collage of photographs portraying heterosexual and homosexual intercourse, sodomy, and masturbation that had been taken from a government report on obscenity. But today, as Frank Rich reported in *The New York Times Magazine* last May [2002] the porn industry—much of it hard-core—generates at least $10 billion per year in revenues for more than 70,000 websites, porn networks, pay-per-view and rental movies, cable and satellite television, and magazine publishers. The 700 million porn rentals per year include, as Rich put it, "a market as diverse as America," in-

2. *Hamling v. United States*, 1974

cluding tattooed performers for the college-age crowd, geriatric porn for older viewers, interracial videos that are popular in the South, and outdoor sex for the Sunbelt. Indeed, two years ago [in 2000], when a local video retailer in Utah was prosecuted for peddling hard-core pornography, he successfully argued that his products were consistent with what his neighbors were watching on pay-per-view.

Internet Regulation Suppresses Speech

Speech that is appropriate for adults, like a discussion of rapes in prison or genital mutilation, may not be appropriate for young children—nevertheless, the Internet cannot be limited to what is only appropriate for them.

In the Supreme Court's 1997 decision concerning the constitutionality of the Communications Decency Act, Justice John Paul Stevens wrote: "In order to deny minors access to potentially harmful speech, the CDA effectively suppresses a large amount of speech that adults have a constitutional right to receive and to address to one another. That burden on adult speech is unacceptable if less restrictive alternatives would be at least as effective in achieving the legitimate purpose that the statute was enacted to serve."

Charles Levendosky, *Casper Star-Tribune*, January 17, 1999.

In other words, consumption patterns reveal Stevens's notion that hard-core pornography is considered patently offensive for adults, in even the most conservative communities in the United States, to be 30 years out-of-date. Unlike the Supreme Court, the porn industry has developed a rating system that classifies material with clinical precision, ranging from x (soft-core) to xx (hard-core) to xxx (ouch!). Now that xxx porn has proliferated across the country—thanks to the Web and to satellite television—the '70s effort to distinguish between the hard-core obscenity in *Hamling*, which could be banned for everyone, and the soft-core pornography in *Playboy*, which had to be protected for adults, has been doomed by the reality of the marketplace. It's no longer possible to argue that hard-core websites are patently offensive to the average American adult, or that soft-core websites are offensive to the average American teenager, since both are enthusiastic consumers. . . .

The truth is that the Supreme Court's entire approach to pornography and obscenity has become a titanic surrender to the implausible. In the '60s, at the dawn of the sexual revolution, the Court struggled valiantly to preserve Victorian definitions of obscenity that relied on some kind of moral consensus about what kind of sexual depictions were beyond the pale. But in the twenty-first century, for better or worse, this moral consensus has collapsed—both at the local and the national level, for adults and teenagers alike. As a result, Congress and the Supreme Court are forced to justify their efforts to regulate porn by invoking the hypothetical possibility of secondary effects—such as harm to minors or the prevention of crime—that aren't remotely borne out by the available evidence.

Technological Alternatives to Laws

Many people disapprove of the explosion of porn on the Internet and understandably want to protect children from it. But in an age when community values have fractured, the law is too clumsy an instrument to regulate sexual expression on the Web. Happily, there are technological alternatives that recognize the diversity of contemporary American values while respecting privacy and free expression. As a bipartisan commission reported to Congress two years ago [in 2000], increasingly sophisticated Internet filtering mechanisms allow individual parents to decide what kind of material they consider appropriate without imposing their views on others. If the Court continues to believe it can precisely calibrate American morality when it reviews COPA in the future, it may unleash a wave of federal censorship that will have little impact on the proliferation of pornography but could wreak havoc on the Internet as a raucous marketplace for free speech.

"Aided by the Internet . . . , online communities with their own publishing tools and networks are redefining news."

Internet Journalism Will Transform the Media Industry

Paul Andrews

The Internet has given hundreds of thousands of people the opportunity to publish their views in personal websites and "weblogs" (online journals) that can be read by other computer users. In the following viewpoint journalist Paul Andrews argues that newspapers and other traditional media institutions are being usurped by individuals and online communities who use the Internet to publish news and commentary. More and more people are getting their news and information from independent websites rather than newspapers or other traditional media sources. He concludes that while personal websites will not completely replace traditional media, they will give voice to those outside the mainstream and serve as an effective way of criticizing faulty or biased reporting in the mainstream mass media. Andrews is a technology reporter for *U.S. News & World Report* and a columnist for the *Seattle Times*.

As you read, consider the following questions:

1. What examples of Internet journalism does Andrews describe?
2. What observation does the author make about media coverage of the terrorist attacks of September 11, 2001?
3. How have newspapers responded to the growing popularity of personal websites?

M arcia Barton does not consider herself a journalist by any stretch of the definition.

The retired Seattle community college instructor "publishes" an environment and politics newsletter featuring commentary and links to stories around the Web—especially those that highlight the follies of the Bush administration. She sends it out almost daily to about a dozen friends.

"I don't think of it as journalism as much as nagging them with alternative points of view," says Barton, who draws from BBC, *The Guardian*, *The Nation*, Democrats.com and Commondreams.org, among others.

Rusty Foster has no idea how he wound up in the information business. A physics and film studies major at William & Mary, Foster turned a programming hobby into an experimental online community site called Kuro5in (pronounced "cur-OH-shin," a homonym for "corrosion" and thus a play on Foster's first name. The Japanese translation—"black heart"—is "cool" but irrelevant, Foster says).

Kuro5in offers the ultimate democratic editorial process: Impromptu discussion groups form around thoughtful postings mostly spun off the news. Regulars rate postings for quality, accuracy and depth. The site draws 100,000 regular readers.

"At its best, the site ends up being really good journalism," says Foster, who runs things from an island 2.5 miles off the coast of Maine. "At its worst, it's just bad op-ed."

Online Communities

Barton and Foster both operate in a journalistic gray zone corporate media can't quite figure out. They are self-made publishers who create more than content: They're building interactive communities that "meet" online to share their thoughts on the news, often writing polished commentary and connect-the-dot essays that pull together news on a topic from various sources.

Stories that are the end result of the news process in traditional media are just the starting point for online communities, which spin off discussions full of context, historical background, conjecture and related links.

Web entrepreneur Jacob Shwirtz dubs the process a "digital campfire." His site, GAZM.org, is "all about giving people a platform to share whatever creative, artistic, intellectual pursuits they're interested in." Swarms of Web users at GAZM alight on a topic du jour, then move on to something new the next day.

Once dominated by anonymous flamers and yahoos, many community news sites now boast contributors with obvious expertise and writing talent. Kuro5in's process of authentication, modeled after the techie site Slashdot.org, ensures a certain credibility and enhances the original report or analysis through its intensive feedback loop. A posting will gain dozens, even hundreds, of commentaries, each enhancing, clarifying and amplifying the original content.

"The end result is an understanding and depth that just is not possible in traditional one-direction journalism," Kuro5in's Foster notes.

Influencing Traditional Media

As their identity, audience, credibility and influence grow, online communities also are breaking news on their own, seeding traditional media reporting.

"I'm about two weeks ahead of *The New York Times*," says Ur-blogger Dave Winer, CEO of UserLand Software and proprietor of one of the Web's earliest and most popular blogs, Scripting News.

The longtime Silicon Valley programmer turned Web evangelist can cite numerous instances where his Weblog, Scripting News, has beaten and/or seeded major news media on technology trends and breakthroughs.

For years Winer has criticized major media as "BigPubs" and "BigCos," unable to "get" the emerging open-software technological trends and viewpoints he champions. But a funny thing happened in April: *The New York Times*, the Cadillac of BigPubs, partnered with Winer to provide content feeds to users of UserLand's Radio blogging software. The deal "was just the tip of the iceberg," Winer says. "Things are really going to explode."

While he won't discuss details, he hints that other, bigger pacts are in the offing—though not necessarily with traditional news publications.

Something is happening here, Mr. Jones, even if we aren't sure what it is.

Aided by the Internet and personal-computer software, online communities with their own publishing tools and networks are redefining news in the 21st Century.

Winer and Foster both call what they do journalism—Barton's not quite ready to make that claim about her informal newsletter.

Weblogs and Reporting the News

Until [the September 11, 2001, terrorist attacks] most mainstream journalists would have laughed at the suggestion that blog sites might be doing journalism. Now they're not so sure.

While TV stations replayed ad nauseum footage of the plane colliding with the tower—and while most newspapers were still running sketchy wire reports—Weblogs throughout Manhattan provided raw feeds from street level.

Able to post text, photos and video almost immediately, blogs easily outshone anything major media could provide. "For the first 48 hours after the bombing, Weblogs were the best source of news available, hands-down," said Foster.

September 11 earned the "amateurs" some respect. Today, journalists—the mainstream ones—find themselves asking questions they rarely contemplated before 9/11: *Are* bloggers journalists? Are these guys *competition?* . . .

Competing with Newspapers

Big Media might just ignore these independent publishers if it weren't for one thing: They're attracting eyeballs—getting clicks and page views that newspapers and other media companies are looking to claim for themselves.

Kuro5in generates 6.5 million page views a month. Winer—whose wide-ranging site mixes tech, politics, culture and Winer's personal musings—draws around 10,000 consistent readers.

There are an estimated 500,000 Weblogs; most attract a few dozen to a few thousand regular readers. These news sites are playing to a vast and growing Internet audience—150 million in the U.S. and 500 million worldwide.

Even as the Web news audience is growing, newspaper circulation is on the depressing end of a 30-year decline: The most recent Audit Bureau of Circulations survey showed circulation was down by .6 percent over six months ending March 31 [2002].

Many of those lost readers are going to the flashy new competitor: The Internet. Surveys show that as many as 20 percent of online users turn to the Internet as their primary news source.

Mainstream media take some comfort in the fact that most people go to newspaper sites for local news, but that could change: Software is getting better at creating personalized news feeds that reflect readers' needs—giving readers a way to get the news they want without visiting newspaper Web sites.

The Digital Media Revolution

At a very fundamental level, the Big Content companies don't understand the revolution that is happening in the digital media realm. They still see us as *consumers* only capable of digesting their offerings and handing over money. They really don't seem to understand that the reason we are buying PCs, video cameras, digital cameras, broadband connections and the like is that we want to create and share our creations. The quality of "amateur" content is exploding at the same time that Big Media companies are going through one of their all-time lows in music and television creativity. No wonder we're spending more time with our PCs than we are with our TVs.

Jonathan Peterson, quoted in "Media Feudalism Under Siege," Techcentralstation.com, December 11, 2002.

And search engines like Google are making it easier to find breaking news at alternative blog sites—drawing referrals away from the mainstream news sites.

With an eye on the potential threat—and the potential to increase audience online—many in the $55 billion newspaper industry are hustling to improve their Web sites; some are opening the door to more interaction with readers online.

Winer says his deal with *The New York Times*—which does not even publish e-mail addresses of its reporters—is a "major breakthrough.". . .

Other newspapers, notably the *Washington Post*, are offering online chats with leading columnists in a sort of talk-radio online format.

MSNBC.com—the Web's most popular news site—added two blogs to its content lineup this week [in May 2002]: Alan Boyle's Cosmic Log (science and technology) and Michael Moran's foreign affairs blog. A handful of other professional journalists have added Weblogs to their reporting duties, although the number is still tiny.

Other online news mechanisms, from mailing lists to discussion groups to hybrids like Kuro5in and GAZM, have found little traction among traditional media.

Will Blogs Replace Mainstream Media?

Bloggers and interactive news communities may eventually further infiltrate the mainstream media; as yet, no one's suggesting they will ever replace it.

As veteran journalist Murray Fromson put it at the University of Southern California's online journalism conference in March [2002], "without newspapers and networks, who will cover a war in Afghanistan?"

Fromson, the former head of USC's journalism department, has a point: Online communities, no matter what their size and reach, rely on traditional news outlets for their core information.

As for covering the war in Afghanistan with Weblogs—well, not yet, perhaps. But they are becoming an important check and balance to an industry that previously had very little oversight.

I was reminded of Fromson's comment recently after the assassination of Dutch prime minister candidate Pim Fortuyn. American newspapers, locked into the binary way of casting domestic politics, referred to Fortuyn as a right-wing candidate. But he was openly gay and a former Marxist and who espoused a number of progressive causes. The right-wing label came from his advocacy of immigration restrictions—a not unreasonable stance in Europe's most overcrowded country.

I looked through several newspapers for an explanation of Fortuyn's politics that confronted such obvious contradictions. I finally found the answer in a Weblog authored by Adam Curry, the former MTV "VJ" who lives in Amsterdam.

Full of knowledgeable asides, links to other blogs and commentaries on published reports, Curry put the tragedy in subtle and intelligent perspective, far outstripping anything conventional U.S. media reported.

In the long run, online communities and pundits like Curry may help strengthen journalism by adding this kind of nuance to the black-and-white reports the BigCos routinely produce.

Ultimately, the mainstream media will likely continue to cover enfranchised sources, and online media will continue to empower the disenfranchised while keeping the pros accountable by dinging them for every instance of superficial or careless reporting.

The end result—until the first blogger or Kuro5in contributor shows up in a White House briefing or Afghanistan reporter pool, at least—will be an uneasy symbiosis of the two organisms, where host and parasite feed off each other interchangeably.

"The Internet's early promise as a medium where text, audio, video and data can be freely exchanged . . . is increasingly being relegated to history's dustbin."

The Media Industry Threatens to Stifle the Promise of the Internet

Jeff Chester and Steven Rosenfeld

In the following viewpoint Jeff Chester and Steven Rosenfeld argue that large media and telecommunications companies are trying to creating an Internet in which they can control content, monitor usage, and compel people to pay for Internet access and information. Public policy priorities such as free speech and the dissemination of views from nonprofit groups are not being given enough attention by policy makers, they conclude. Chester is executive director of the Center for Digital Democracy, an organization that works to preserve the openness and diversity of the Internet and promote the development of noncommercial, public interest programming. Rosenfeld is a senior editor for *Tom Paine.com*, an electronic public interest journal.

As you read, consider the following questions:
1. Why has the development of next-generation digital television been delayed, according to the authors?
2. What historical analogy regarding the actions of media corporations do Chester and Rosenfeld make?

Ever stop to wonder what is really happening to the Internet these days? The crackdown by the music industry on illegal downloading[1] tells just part of the story. . . . The thousands of lawsuits are not just about ensuring record companies and artists get the royalties they deserve. They're part of a larger plan to fundamentally change the way the Internet works.

From Congress to Silicon Valley, the nation's largest communication and entertainment conglomerates—and software firms that want their business—are seeking to restructure the Internet, to charge people for high-speed uses that are now free and to monitor content in an unprecedented manner. This is not just to see if users are swapping copyrighted CDs or DVDs, but to create digital dossiers for their own marketing purposes.

All told, this is the business plan of America's handful of telecom giants—the phone, cable, satellite, wireless and entertainment companies that now bring high-speed Internet access to most Americans. Their ability to meter Internet use, monitor Internet content and charge according to those metrics is how they are positioning themselves for the evolving Internet revolution.

The Internet's early promise as a medium where text, audio, video and data can be freely exchanged and the public interest can be served is increasingly being relegated to history's dustbin. Today, the part of the Net that is public and accessible is shrinking, while the part of the Net tied to round-the-clock billing is poised to grow exponentially.

Proposed Levels of Service

One front in the corporate high-tech takeover of the Internet can be seen in Congress. On July 21 [2003], the House Subcommittee on Telecommunications and the Internet held a hearing on the "Regulatory Status of Broadband." There, a coalition that included Amazon.com, Microsoft, Yahoo, Apple, Disney and others, told Congress that Internet service providers (ISPs) should be able to impose volume-

---

1. In 2003 the Recording Industry Association of America (RIAA) filed civil lawsuits against hundreds of people that it claimed were illegally distributing music files over the Internet.

based fee structures, based on bits transmitted per month. This is part of a behind-the-scenes struggle by the Net's content providers and retailers to cut deals with the ISPs so that each sector will have unimpaired access to consumers and can maximize profits.

The industry coalition spoke of "tiered" service, where consumers would be charged according to "gold, silver and bronze" levels of bandwidth use. The days where lawmakers once spoke about eradicating the "Digital Divide" in America has come full circle. Under the scenario presented by the lobbyists, people on fixed incomes would have to accept a stripped-down Internet, full of personally targeted advertising. Other users could get a price break if they receive bundled content—news, music, games—from one telecom or media company. Anybody interested in other "non-mainstream" news, software or higher-volume usage, could pay for the privilege. The panel's response was warm, suggesting that the industry should work this out with little federal intrusion. That approach has already been embraced by the industry-friendly Federal Communications Commission.

Meanwhile, in the courts, there has been a rash of new litigation spurred by the Recording Industry Association of America (RIAA)'s pursuit of people who have illegally shared copyrighted music. The music industry no doubt hopes to discourage file-swapping piracy, and some big telecom companies, such as SBC Communications, have counter-sued, saying they will protect their clients' privacy. While that's good public relations, there's more to this story as well. Telecoms, like most big corporations, don't want other businesses, let alone the government, interfering in their operations—so there's plenty of reasons to counter-sue—even if the record companies and telecoms have parallel stakes in privatizing the Net.

Monitoring Internet Content

But there's also a technologically insidious element to this side of the story. The software now exists to track and monitor Internet content on a scale and to a degree that previously hasn't been possible. The RIAA is taking people to court because it *has* the technology to track illegal Internet

The Internet and Corporate Control

As the corporate media domination of Internet "content" crystallizes, the claims of the Internet utopians are beginning to get downsized. We are probably going to hear less about how the Internet will invigorate media competition and more about how since anyone can start a website, we should all just shut up and be happy consumers. But, in the big scheme of things, having the ability to launch a website at a nominal expense is only slightly more compelling than saying we have no grounds of concern about monopoly newspapers because anyone can write up a newsletter and wave it in their front window or hand it out to their neighbors.

Viable websites for journalism and entertainment need resources and people who earn a living at producing them, precisely what the market has eliminated any chance of developing. Moreover, just having a zillion amateur websites may not be all that impressive. One expert estimates that over 80 percent of all websites fail to show up on any search engines, making them virtually impossible to find, and the situation may only get worse.

Robert McChesney, *Extra!*, March/April 2000.

---

file swapping. This level of content-tracking is the next-generation application of what's been developed to keep children and teenagers from viewing porn at the local library or home. Consider this typical bit of sales arcana from the Web site of Allot Communications, which says its software can track and filter Internet communications and use that analysis to bill consumers.

> Allot Communications provides network traffic management and content filtering solutions for enterprises, IP service providers, and educational institutions. . . . Allot's QoS [quality of service] and service-level agreement enforcement solutions maximize return on investment by managing oversubscription [unintended uses], throttling P2P [peer-to-peer, the music piracy software] traffic and delivering tiered classes of services.

This new world of metering, monitoring and monetizing Internet content has prompted new business ventures, such as cable firms exploring partnerships with the videogame industry, where there's plenty of money to be made in high-volume interactive uses. In fact, the reason Hollywood has delayed the deployment of next-generation digital television, besides their fear of digital piracy, is they have not yet figured out how to impose their pricing model—to extend their current distribution and sales monopoly.

The Public Interest

Of course, the last concern in corporate boardrooms and Congress is how the privatization of the Net will affect free speech and the public interest. Just as C-Span and public broadcasting were crumbs thrown to the public the last time new communications technologies were developed, there's been little talk about insulating public-interest uses from a more 'metered' Internet.

There is undoubtedly a legitimate business case to be made for having people pay for emerging high-bandwidth uses, but whether people will be charged to see streamed videos of political candidates or public meetings is another matter. Moreover, users need to know what part of the Net will be public and accessible and what part will be billed to credit cards—and this is unclear.

While there needs to be a balance between private sector goals and public policy needs, that's hardly a topic of discussion on the Internet's frontline. Currently, America's media giants are planning the equivalent of a 19th-century land grab in cyberspace to ensure they will profit mightily in the 21st century. Metering data transmissions and monitoring content is how they will get there. And the tools and political climate to achieve this are here.

This century's new media giants are now working with Congress, Federal Communications Commission chairman Michael Powell and their industry partners to transform the Internet. The only open question is whether the public will influence this transformation before it's too late.

Periodical Bibliography

The following articles have been selected to supplement the diverse views presented in this chapter.

Ian Austen — "Meet the New Web. Same as the Old Web," *New York Times*, September 28, 2000.

Jeffrey Chester and Gary O. Larson — "Something Old, Something New: Media Policy in Digital Age," *Nation*, January 7, 2002.

David Gelernter — "The Next Great American Newspaper," *Weekly Standard*, June 23, 2003.

John Maxwell Hamilton and Eric Jenner — "The New Foreign Correspondence," *Foreign Affairs*, September/October 2003.

John Leo — "Flogged by Bloggers," *U.S. News & World Report*, August 5, 2002.

Robert W. McChesney — "The Titanic Sails On," *Extra!*, March/April 2000.

Robert W. McChesney and John Nichols — "Our Media, Not Theirs," *In These Times*, April 14, 2003.

Jim Milliot — "Supreme Court to Hear COPA Appeal: First Amendment Rights on the Web," *Publishers Weekly*, October 20, 2003.

Nieman Reports — "Weblogs and Journalism," Fall 2003.

Barb Palser — "Does the Net Counter Consolidation? How the Web May or May Not Live Up to the FCC's 'Diversity of Choice' Claim," *American Journalism Review*, August/September 2003.

Glenn Harlan Reynolds — "Weblogs and Journalism: Back to the Future? A Blogger Predicts That Weblogs Might Push Big Media Back to Better News Reporting," *Nieman Reports*, Fall 2003.

Frances Smith — "Protecting Kids on the Internet," *Consumers' Research Magazine*, January 1999.

Andrew Ross Sorkin — "Building a Web Media Empire on a Daily Dose of Fresh Links," *New York Times*, November 17, 2003.

Lawrence H. Tribe — "The Internet vs. the First Amendment," *New York Times*, April 28, 1999.

Elsa Wenzel — "Will Big Media Choke the Net?" *PC World*, June 13, 2003.

For Further Discussion

Chapter 1

1. Tyler Cohen argues that the media are trying to give customers what they want, nothing more. After reading the viewpoints of Cohen and Sheila Gribben Liaugminas, do you believe that the media have responsibilities beyond attracting and pleasing their paying customers? What might such responsibilities be? Do consumers of media have responsibilities as well? Explain.

2. E.J. Dionne makes a distinction between social and cultural issues, in which he contends the media may be liberal, and economic issues, in which the media favor conservative views. What examples of bias in each area does he provide? Do you believe such a distinction helps in analyzing media bias? Why or why not? Is a similar distinction made in the viewpoints by Pat Buchanan, William McGowan, and others in the chapter, or are cultural and economic issues lumped together? Explain.

3. Pamela Newkirk uses stories from her own experience as a journalist in her argument that racial prejudice exists in the media. William McGowan cites stories from other journalists. Which stories do you find more convincing? Why?

4. After reading the viewpoints of Edward Monks, Katherine Mangu-Ward, and Joseph Farah, do you believe that the media should be required by the government to provide opposing views, or should the government stay out of telling the media what to say? Defend your answer.

5. After reading the viewpoints in this chapter, do you believe journalists should continue to strive for objectivity, or is objectivity simply impossible and journalists should instead just be honest and open about their prejudices and biases? Defend your answer using examples and arguments from the viewpoints.

Chapter 2

1. Mark Crispin Miller's essay includes strong criticisms directed personally against FCC chairman Michael Powell. Can such attacks be dismissed as not relevant to the issues being discussed, or do they strengthen Miller's general points? Defend your answer.

2. Adam Thierer and Clyde Wayne Crews Jr. dismiss fears of media monopolies by arguing that dissatisfied Americans "are always free to establish new media outlets." Do you believe this is a valid argument that allays the concerns expressed by Miller? Explain why or why not.

3. James Gattuso argues that Americans enjoy more diversity and competition in the media than ever before. What facts and arguments does he provide to support his assertion? Do you agree with his view that such diversity makes FCC rules on media ownership outdated? Explain your answers.

4. Ted Turner is himself a media entrepreneur who helped create a large media company (which was then sold to an even larger corporation). Does his background lend greater credence to his arguments about media consolidation? Why or why not?

5. Bill Park provides much background on his personal and professional history with radio. Are his accounts of the history of the radio industry relevant to arguments over radio deregulation today? Explain your answer.

6. Why might Lowry Mays have an interest in convincing Congress of his arguments that radio deregulation has helped the industry, given his position as head of Clear Channel? Does his personal interest in the debate compromise the validity of his arguments, in your opinion? Why or why not?

Chapter 3

1. Both the Senate Judiciary Committee staff and Richard Rhodes cite outside sources and experts in their opposing arguments about the effects of media violence on the young. After reading both viewpoints, how would you rate the respective credentials of the outside experts the authors use. Does the "expert" standing of sources matter more or less than the substance of the arguments put forth, in your view? Explain your answer.

2. After reading the viewpoints by Ramesh Ponnuru and Maurice Carroll, do you believe that the media are too dependent on polls for gathering and reporting information? Would you be more or less interested in media stories about elections if polls were not used? Defend your answers.

3. David J. Hanson uses a mocking tone in his article, calling a gathering of opponents of alcohol advertising a "junk science congregation" of "true believers." What might be the goal of such a style of writing, in your view? After reading his viewpoint and that of George A. Hacker, do you agree with Hanson's assessment? Explain.

Chapter 4

1. Both Neil Morton and Mark Briggs make predictions on what the newspapers will look like in the future. In what areas are the

predictions similar? In what areas do they diverge? Which predictions do you find more convincing? Explain.

2. Jeffrey Rosen argues that no national consensus exists on what constitutes obscenity, making regulation of Internet pornography impossible. Could the poll results described by the organization Morality in Media be used to refute Rosen's argument? Explain how or why not.

3. Paul Andrews uses the metaphor of an "uneasy symbiosis" between "host and parasite" to describe the evolving relationship between personal websites and mainstream media. Do you believe his analogy is apt? Explain your answer.

4. Jeff Chester and Steven Rosenfeld argue that media companies are trying to restructure the Internet to exert greater control over and derive more profit from it. What arguments do they make that such restructuring is a bad thing—or do they simply assume that it is? What are your own views on the role of media corporations and the Internet?

Organizations to Contact

The editors have compiled the following list of organizations concerned with issues debated in this book. The descriptions are derived from materials provided by the organizations. All have publications or information available for interested readers. The list was compiled on the date of publication of the present volume; the information provided here may change. Be aware that many organizations take several weeks or longer to respond to inquiries, so allow as much time as possible.

Accuracy in Media (AIM)
4455 Connecticut Ave. NW, Suite 330, Washington, DC 20008
(202) 364-4401 • fax: (202) 364-4090
e-mail: arl@aim.org • website: www.aim.org
AIM is a conservative media watchdog organization. It researches public complaints on errors of fact made by the news media and requests that such errors be corrected publicly. It publishes the semimonthly *AIM Report* and a weekly syndicated newspaper column.

American Society of Newspaper Editors (ASNE)
11690B Sunrise Valley Dr., Reston, VA 20101-1409
(703) 453-1122 • fax: (703) 453-1133
e-mail: asne@asne.org • website: www.asne.org
ASNE is a membership organization of editors in charge of major policy decisions at American daily newspapers. Articles from its magazine *American Editor* and other information on its projects on newsroom diversity and other areas of concern to the media can be found on its website.

Center for Media and Public Affairs (CMPA)
2100 L St. NW, Suite 300, Washington, DC 20037
(202) 223-2942 • fax: (202) 872-4014
website: www.cmpa.com
CMPA is a nonpartisan research organization that studies the media's treatment of social and political affairs and uses surveys to measure the media's influence on public opinion. It publishes the *Media Monitor* newsletter and various studies of the media, including *Media Coverage of Global Warming* and *What the People Want from the Press.*

Center for Media Literacy
3101 Ocean Park Blvd., #200, Santa Monica, CA 90405
(310) 581-0260 • fax: (310) 581-0270
e-mail: cml@medialit.org • website: www.medialit.org

The center is a nonprofit national educational organization that promotes media literacy education as a way to help students develop critical thinking skills to analyze and create media content. Its website features articles, reports, and teaching kits about media literacy, including archived articles from the magazine *Media & Values*. The organization also publishes the newsletter *Connect*.

Fairness and Accuracy in Reporting (FAIR)
112 W. 27th St., New York, NY 10001
(212) 633-6700 • fax: (212) 727-7668
e-mail: fair@fair.org • website: www.fair.org

FAIR is a liberal media watchdog organization that seeks to expose conservative bias in the media. It publishes the bimonthly *EXTRA!* magazine and features numerous articles and analyses on its website.

Federal Communications Commission (FCC)
445 12th St. SW, Washington, DC 20554
(888) 225-5322 • fax: (866) 418-0232
e-mail: fccinfo@fcc.gov • website: www.fcc.gov

The FCC is an independent government agency responsible for regulating interstate and international communications by radio, television, wire, satellite, and cable. The FCC is required to review the educational programming efforts of the networks. It publishes various reports, updates, and reviews that can be accessed online at their website.

Media Institute
1800 N. Kent St., Suite 1130, Arlington, VA 22209
(703) 243-5060 • fax: (703) 243-2453
e-mail: info@mediainstitute.org
website: www.mediainstitute.org

The Media Institute is a nonprofit research foundation that specializes in communications policy and First Amendment issues. It supports deregulation of the media and communications industry and works to foster freedom of speech and excellence in journalism. Its publications include *The First Amendment and the Media* and *Alcohol Advertising on the Air*.

Media Research Center (MRC)
325 S. Patrick St., Alexandria, VA 22314
(703) 683-9733 • fax: (703) 683-9736
e-mail: mrc@mediaresearch.org
website: www.mediaresearch.org

The center is a conservative media watchdog organization concerned with what it perceives to be a liberal bias in the news and entertainment media. It monitors and reports on problems in the media in its newsletters *Media Watch* and *Notable Quotables* and on its website.

Morality in the Media (MIM)
475 Riverside Dr., Suite 239, New York, NY 10115
(212) 870-3222 • fax: (212) 870-2765
e-mail: mim@moralityinmedia.org
website: www.moralityinmedia.org

Established in 1962, MIM is a national, not-for-profit interfaith organization that works to combat obscenity and to uphold decency standards in the media. It maintains the National Obscenity Law Center, a clearinghouse of legal materials, and conducts public information programs to involve concerned citizens. It publishes the *Morality in Media* newsletter and the handbook *Stranger in the House.*

National Coalition Against Censorship
275 Seventh Ave., New York, NY 10001
(212) 807-6222 • fax: (212) 807-6245
e-mail: ncac@ncac.org • website: www.ncac.org

The coalition of nonprofit groups opposes censorship in any form, believing it to be against the First Amendment right to freedom of speech. It works to educate the public about the dangers of censorship, including censorship of violence on television and in movies and music. The coalition publishes *Censorship News* four times a year and reports such as *The Cyber-Library: Legal and Policy Issues Facing Public Libraries in the High-Tech Era.*

National Institute on Media and the Family
606 24th Ave. South, Suite 606, Minneapolis, MN 55454
(888) 672-5427 • fax: (612) 672-4113
website: www.mediafamily.org

The National Institute on Media and the Family is a national resource for research, education, and information about the impact of media on children and families. It provides information about media products and their likely impact on children to parents and other adults so they can make informed choices. It publishes the *Mediawise* newsletter and provides fact sheets on media violence and other topics on its website.

Parents Television Council (PTC)
707 Wilshire Blvd., Suite 2075, Los Angeles, CA 90017
(213) 629-9255
website: www.parentstv.org

PTC works to promote positive, family-oriented television programming. It publishes the PTC *Insider* newsletter, reports including *The Blue Tube: Foul Language on Prime Time Network TV* and guides and ratings of television programs and motion pictures.

Pew Research Center for the People and the Press
1150 18th St. NW, Suite 975, Washington, DC 20036
(202) 293-3126 • fax: (202) 293-2569
e-mail: mailprc@people-press.org
website: http://people-press.org

Formerly known as the Times Mirror Center for the People & the Press, the center is an independent opinion research group that conducts opinion surveys and studies on the attitudes of the public, the media, and politicians toward political and media issues. It publishes numerous research reports, including *Strong Opposition to Media Cross-Ownership Emerges.*

Society for the Eradication of Television (SET)
Box 10491, Oakland, CA 94610-0491
(510) 763-8712
e-mail: set.info@webwm.com • website: www.webwm.com

SET members oppose television and encourage others to stop all television viewing. The society believes television "retards the inner life of human beings, destroys human interaction, and squanders time." It distributes articles and books including *REALIZATIONS: Television, also Known as "Commercial Mass Culture."* Articles about television from various sources can also be found on its website.

Websites

International Press Institute (IPI)
www.freemedia.at/index1.html

IPI is a global network of editors, media executives, and leading journalists from news agencies in over one hundred nations.

Mediachannel.org

www.mediachannel.org

Mediachannel.org is a public interest website on global media issues. It features criticism and investigative reporting about the media from hundreds of organizations worldwide.

Media Transparency

www.mediatransparency.org

The website, a creation of a Minnesota-based investigative journalist, documents links between conservative philanthropies and the organizations and people they fund, and their influence in the media and how it covers stories.

Media Watch

www.pbs.org/newshour/media

Part of the companion website to the Public Broadcasting System (PBS) *NewsHour* television program.

The Merchants of Cool

www.pbs.org/wgbh/pages/frontline/shows/cool

A companion website to the 2001 *Frontline* television documentary by the Public Broadcasting System that examines the relationships between the media, marketing, and popular culture among America's teens.

Pressthink

http://journalism.nyu.edu/pubzone/weblogs/pressthink

The creation of press critic and author Jay Rosen, Pressthink is an ongoing website that analyzes media trends and debates, including essays on media bias and how the Internet is changing the practice of journalism.

Who Owns What?

www.cjr.org/tools/owners

A continuously updated online guide by the *Columbia Journalism Review* on what properties the major media companies own.

Bibliography of Books

Alan B. Albarran and David Goff, eds.	*Understanding the Web.* Ames: Iowa State University Press, 2000.
Eric Alterman	*What Liberal Media? The Truth About Bias and the News.* New York: Basic Books, 2003.
David Arant, ed.	*Perspectives: Ethics, Issues and Controversies in Mass Media.* St. Paul, MN: Coursewise, 1999.
John Arden	*America's Meltdown: The Lowest-Common-Denominator Society.* Westport, CT: Praeger, 2003.
Ben H. Bagdikian	*The New Media Monopoly.* Boston: Beacon Press, 2004.
Arthur Berger	*The Agent in the Agency: Media, Popular Culture, and Everyday Life in America.* Cresskill, NJ: Hampton Press, 2003.
Noam Chomsky and Edward S. Herman	*Manufacturing Consent: The Political Economy of the Mass Media.* New York: Pantheon Books, 2002.
Roy Peter Clark and Cole C. Campbell, eds.	*The Value and Craft of American Journalism.* Gainesville: University Press of Florida, 2002.
Benjamin M. Compaine and Douglas Gomery	*Who Owns the Media?* Mahwah, NJ: Lawrence Erlbaum Associates, 2000.
Joe Conason	*Big Lies: The Right-Wing Propaganda Machine and How It Distorts the Truth.* New York: Thomas Dunne Books, 2003.
Don H. Corrigan	*The Public Journalism Movement in America: Evangelists in the Newsroom.* Westport, CT: Praeger, 1999.
William Cote and Roger Simpson	*Covering Violence.* New York: Columbia University Press, 2000.
David Croteau	*The Business of Media.* Thousand Oaks, CA: Pine Forge Press, 2001.
Everette E. Dennis and Edward C. Pease, eds.	*The Media in Black and White.* Rutgers, NJ: Transaction Books, 1997.
Roland De Wolk	*Introduction to Online Journalism.* Boston: Allyn and Bacon, 2001.
Leonard Downie Jr. and Robert G. Kaiser	*The News About the News.* New York: Knopf, 2002.
James Fallows	*Breaking the News: How the Media Undermine American Democracy.* New York: Pantheon Books, 1996.

Jib Fowles	*The Case for Television Violence.* Thousand Oaks, CA: Sage, 1999.
Roy F. Fox	*Mediaspeak: Three American Voices.* Westport, CT: Praeger, 2001.
Jonathan L. Freedman	*Media Violence and Its Effect on Aggression: Assessing the Scientific Evidence.* Toronto: University of Toronto Press, 2002.
Herbert J. Gans	*Democracy and the News.* New York: Oxford University Press, 2003.
Eytan Gilboa, ed.	*Media and Conflict: Framing Issues, Making Policy, Shaping Opinions.* Ardsley, NY: Transnational, 2002.
Todd Gitlin	*Media Unlimited: How the Torrents and Sound Overwhelm Our Lives.* New York: Metropolitan Books, 2001.
Theodore L. Glasser, ed.	*The Idea of Public Journalism.* New York: Guilford Press, 1999.
Bernard Goldberg	*Arrogance: Rescuing America from the Media Elite.* New York: Warner Books, 2003.
Bernard Goldberg	*Bias: A CBS Insider Exposes How the Media Distort the News.* Washington, DC: Regnery, 2002.
Felix Gutierrez, Clint Wilson, and Lena Chao	*Racism, Sexism, and the Media: The Rise of Class Communication in Multicultural America.* Thousand Oaks, CA: Sage, 2003.
Michele Hilmes	*Only Connect: A Cultural History of Broadcasting in the United States.* Belmont, CA: Wadsworth, 2002.
Henry Jenkins and David Thorburn, eds.	*Democracy and the New Media.* Cambridge, MA: MIT Press, 2003.
Gerard Jones	*Killing Monsters: Why Children Need Fantasy, Super Heroes, and Make-Believe Violence.* New York: Basic Books, 2002.
Yahya R. Kamalipour and Theresa Carilli, eds.	*Cultural Diversity and the U.S. Media.* Albany: State University of New York, 1998.
Kevin Kawamoto	*Media and Society in a Digital Age.* Boston: Allyn and Bacon, 2003.
Matthew Kerbel	*If It Bleeds, It Leads: An Anatomy of Television News.* Boulder, CO: Westview Press, 2000.
Bill Kovach and Tom Rosenstiel	*Warp Speed: America in the Age of Mixed Media.* New York: Century Foundation, 1999.

Hugh Mackay	*Media Mania: Why Our Fear of the Modern Media Is Misplaced.* Sydney, Australia: UNSW Press, 2002.
William McGowan	*Coloring the News.* San Francisco: Encounter Books, 2001.
John C. Merrill, Peter J. Gade, and Frederick R. Blevens	*Twilight of Press Freedom: The Rise of People's Journalism.* Mahwah, NJ: Lawrence Erlbaum Associates, 2001.
David T.Z. Mindich	*Just the Facts: How Objectivity Came to Define American Journalism.* New York: New York University Press, 1998.
John Nichols and Robert W. McChesney	*It's the Media, Stupid.* New York: Seven Stories Press, 2000.
David L. Paletz	*The Media in American Politics.* New York: Addison-Wesley, 2001.
John V. Pavlik	*Journalism and New Media.* New York: Columbia University Press, 2001.
W. James Potter	*The 11 Myths of Media Violence.* Thousand Oaks, CA: Sage, 2002.
Gene Roberts, ed.	*Leaving Readers Behind: The Age of Corporate Newspapering.* Fayetteville: University of Arkansas Press, 2001.
Jay Rosen	*What Are Journalists For?* New Haven, CT: Yale University Press, 2001.
Daniel W. Rossides	*Communications, Media, and American Society: A Critical Introduction.* Lanham, MD: Rowman & Littlefield, 2003.
Christopher H. Sterling and John Michael Kittross	*Stay Tuned: A Concise History of American Broadcasting.* Mahwah, NJ: Lawrence Erlbaum Associates, 2002.
Elizabeth L. Toth and Linda Aldorry, eds.	*The Gender Challenge to Media: Diverse Voices from the Field.* Cresskill, NJ: Hampton Press, 2001.
Doug Underwood	*From Yahweh to Yahoo!: The Religious Roots of the Secular Press.* Urbana: University of Illinois Press, 2002.

Index

215

89–90

Philadelphia Daily News (newspaper), 48

Plato, 127

Ponnuru, Ramesh, 141

Poston, Ted, 43–44

Powell, Michael, 65, 77, 78, 79, 201
  on media monopolies, 84

Proxmire, William, 58

public interest, media monopolies are harmful to, 79–81

Public Opinion (Lippman), 21, 26

public opinion/public opinion polls
  can be steered by opinion makers, 26
  downside of, 148–49
  on Internet obscenity, 179–80
  on media and juvenile crime, 124–25
  negatively affect the U.S. political process, 141–45
    con, 146–50
  on news coverage, 14
  on perceived dangers of sharks, 120
  on perceptions of bias in media, 18
  see also surveys

Quayle, Dan, 135

racial conflict, media is biased in coverage of, 49–50

radio
  conservative talk, repeal of Fairness Doctrine and rise of, 55–58
  deregulation of media ownership has harmed, 98–106
    con, 107–15
  explosion of formats on, 112
  increase in advertising revenue of, 102–103
  ownership restrictions on, 89

Radio/TV Cross-Ownership Ban, 89

Rather, Dan, 36

Reagan, Michael, 56

Reagan, Ronald, 54

Recording Industry Association of America (RIAA), 198, 199

regulation(s), of media ownership, 88–89
  deregulation has harmed radio, 98–106
  should be lifted, 87–92
    con, 93–97

Republic (Plato), 127

Rhodes, Richard, 131

Robinson, Matthew, 141, 144, 145

Roper Center, 29

Rosen, Jay, 14–15

Rosen, Jeffrey, 183

Rosenfeld, Steven, 197

Ruderman, Gary, 24, 25

Saltzman, Joe, 119

Savage, Michael, 56

Scalia, Antonin, 59

Schaffer, Jan, 15

Schwartz, Douglas, 148

Scripting News (weblog), 192

Senate Committee on the Judiciary, 121

SFX, 106

Shapiro, Bob, 149

Shwirtz, Jacob, 191–92

Smerconsih, Michael, 48

Smith, Craig, 59

Socrates, 127

Sowell, Thomas, 19, 23

Sprafkin, Joyce, 135

Stavitsky, Joe, 139–40

Steel, Ronald, 26

Steiger, Janet, 156

Steinhorn, Leonard, 144

Stevens, John Paul, 186–87, 188

Stonehill, Brian, 130

Supreme Court
  on antipornography laws, 181
  on Child Online Protection Act, 184
  on Fairness Doctrine, 55
  on tobacco advertising, 156

Surgeon General, U.S., report on television violence by, 125

surveys
  on Internet and video game use by children, 129
  on Internet as primary news source, 89–90, 194
  on Internet obscenity, 181–82
  of minorities in newsrooms, 40
  on teen drinking, 155
  on time spent by teens listening to music, 128
  on voting patterns of journalists, 18, 29, 37
  on weapons carried by youths, 122
  see also public opinion/public opinion polls

Telecommunications Act (1996), 71, 79, 89
  trends in radio ownership following, 104

television
  increase in violence on, 123
  ownership restrictions on, 88–89
  sexual content on, 186
  stations, growth in number of, 83–84, 90–91
  studies of violence on, 125–26